"This book is a comprehensive and importa
of justification by faith alone, which is one
tian doctrines and key to understanding the true nature
Schreiner's presentation is informative and lucid, making it one of the best ways for students and others to grasp what justification is and why it matters today as much as ever."

Gerald Bray, Research Professor of Divinity, Beeson Divinity School, Samford University

"There is no doctrine more important to the Christian faith than the doctrine of justification. There is no biblical scholar I'd rather learn this doctrine from than Tom Schreiner. This short book features one of our era's most prominent theologians concisely explaining the very doctrine upon which the church stands or falls. That is more than enough reason to read this book and benefit from it."

Tim Challies, author, *Seasons of Sorrow*

"This wonderfully rich and concise study models how to grasp and explain a central Christian doctrine. Schreiner unfolds the Bible's understanding of justification, the struggle for its preservation through the centuries, and its rediscovery at the Reformation. Rich in exegetical detail and interaction with alternate understandings, this study succeeds magnificently at presenting just what justification is and why it is central to Christian life and thought. In Schreiner's words, 'it gives us assurance, frees us from fear, and awakens praise in our hearts.' A profound yet practical book to study and to treasure!"

Robert W. Yarbrough, Professor of New Testament, Covenant Theological Seminary

"With his characteristic clarity, Schreiner harvests the fruits of his many faithful labors as a New Testament scholar and Christian minister in this introduction to the doctrine of justification. The book ranges widely—covering church history, the biblical material, contemporary challenges, theological formulation, and practical application—but it remains succinct and accessible. Foundational to this brief account is Schreiner's career of careful exegetical and theological study and meditation. He reminds his readers that justification by faith alone is no mere theological quarrel. It is the source of the Christian's assurance, freedom, and joy!"

R. Lucas Stamps, Chair of the Hobbs School of Theology and Ministry, Oklahoma Baptist University

Justification

SHORT STUDIES IN SYSTEMATIC THEOLOGY

Edited by Graham A. Cole and Oren R. Martin

The Attributes of God: An Introduction, Gerald Bray (2021)

The Church: An Introduction, Gregg R. Allison (2021)

The Doctrine of Scripture: An Introduction, Mark D. Thompson (2022)

Faithful Theology: An Introduction, Graham A. Cole (2020)

Glorification: An Introduction, Graham A. Cole (2022)

Justification: An Introduction, Thomas R. Schreiner (2023)

The Person of Christ: An Introduction, Stephen J. Wellum (2021)

The Trinity: An Introduction, Scott R. Swain (2020)

Justification

An Introduction

Thomas R. Schreiner

WHEATON, ILLINOIS

Justification: An Introduction

Published by Crossway
1300 Crescent Street
Wheaton, Illinois 60187

Cover design: Jordan Singer

First printing 2023

Printed in the United States of America

All emphases in Scripture quotations have been added by the author.

Trade paperback ISBN: 978-1-4335-7573-0
ePub ISBN: 978-1-4335-7576-1
PDF ISBN: 978-1-4335-7574-7
Mobipocket ISBN: 978-1-4335-7575-4

Library of Congress Cataloging-in-Publication Data

Names: Schreiner, Thomas R., author.
Title: Justification : an introduction / Thomas R. Schreiner.
Description: Wheaton, Illinois : Crossway, 2023. | Series: Short studies in systematic theology | Includes bibliographical references and index.
Identifiers: LCCN 2022030443 (print) | LCCN 2022030444 (ebook) | ISBN 9781433575730 (hardcover) | ISBN 9781433575747 (pdf) | ISBN 9781433575761 (epub)
Subjects: LCSH: Justification (Christian theology) | Justification (Christian theology)—Biblical teaching.
Classification: LCC BT764.3 .S37 2023 (print) | LCC BT764.3 (ebook) | DDC 234/.7—dc23/eng/20230206
LC record available at https://lccn.loc.gov/2022030443
LC ebook record available at https://lccn.loc.gov/2022030444

Crossway is a publishing ministry of Good News Publishers.

VP 32 31 30 29 28 27 26 25 24 23
15 14 13 12 11 10 9 8 7 6 5 4 3 2 1

Contents

Series Preface

The ancient Greek thinker Heraclitus reputedly said that the thinker has to listen to the essence of things. A series of theological studies dealing with the traditional topics that make up systematic theology needs to do just that. Accordingly, in each of these studies, a theologian addresses the essence of a doctrine. This series thus aims to present short studies in theology that are attuned to both the Christian tradition and contemporary theology in order to equip the church to faithfully understand, love, teach, and apply what God has revealed in Scripture about a variety of topics. What may be lost in comprehensiveness can be gained through what John Calvin, in the dedicatory epistle of his commentary on Romans, called "lucid brevity."

Of course, a thorough study of any doctrine will be longer rather than shorter, as there are two millennia of confession, discussion, and debate with which to interact. As a result, a short study needs to be more selective but deftly so. Thankfully, the contributors to this series have the ability to be brief yet accurate. The key aim is that the simpler is not to morph into the simplistic. The test is whether the topic of a short study, when further studied in depth, requires some unlearning to take place. The simple can be amplified. The simplistic needs to be corrected. As editors, we believe that the volumes in this series pass that test.

While the specific focus varies, each volume (1) introduces the doctrine, (2) sets it in context, (3) develops it from Scripture, (4) draws the various threads together, and (5) brings it to bear on the Christian life. It is our prayer, then, that this series will assist the church to delight in her triune God by thinking his thoughts—which he has graciously revealed in his written word, which testifies to his living Word, Jesus Christ—after him in the powerful working of his Spirit.

Graham A. Cole and Oren R. Martin

Preface

I am grateful to Oren Martin and Graham Cole for inviting me to write this book, and especially to Oren Martin who is my next-door neighbor and a precious friend! My thanks to Drs. Martin and Cole for editing my manuscript and for suggestions for improvement. I am also very grateful for my longtime friend Chris Cowan who did the editing for Crossway and for his keen eye and excellent editing skills. I should add my thanks to Crossway for also publishing this piece and for its faithful ministry in publishing books that are trustworthy and edifying.

I have written often about justification over the years, but I never tire of the topic since it addresses one of the most important issues in life: how can I be free from guilt when I stand before a holy God? This book is not a technical treatment of the doctrine of justification, but I hope readers see the biblical and historical underpinnings for the doctrine of justification. The doctrine should not only be presented, explicated, and defended in longer books but also in sermons, home Bible studies, college and seminary classes, and in books that summarize the main teaching. Many luminaries have preceded me in writing about justification, and I acknowledge my debt and my thanks to all who have taught me about this precious truth both in person and in their writings. Martin Luther was right in claiming that this truth must be regularly taught for the life and health of the church, for once justification by faith alone is assumed, it is quickly forgotten. If we take justification by faith for granted, our eyes will move away from the grace of God and begin to focus on what we do and what we accomplish. Justification reminds us that salvation is God's work, that we have been favored by his love, and that our hope doesn't lie in ourselves but in Christ crucified and risen.

Introduction

Justification isn't merely a doctrinal question but speaks to our relationship with the one true God, concerning how we can stand in the right before him. Hence, it is one of the most important questions in life. The question becomes particularly acute when we realize that we are sinners before a holy God, that our unrighteousness means that there is no reason God should count us as righteous before him. Since we have not obeyed the Lord, we deserve judgment rather than vindication. The Christian gospel, however, proclaims that we can be justified before the Holy One of Israel. The ungodly are declared to be in the right before the divine Judge if they put their faith in Jesus as the crucified and risen one.

The pastoral urgency of justification is evident since it speaks to our relationship with God, but the doctrine of justification raises serious academic and theological questions since it played a fundamental role in the division of the Western church in the sixteenth century. Jesus prayed that the church would be united, that the church would be one (John 17:21, 23), and yet this doctrine caused a great severing in the church, a separation that has continued to this day. Was such a separation worth it? Was it warranted, or did our ancestors, particularly our Reformed ancestors, go astray? One's answer depends on how one understands justification and how important the doctrine is deemed to be. The fracturing of the church is always a tragedy; nevertheless, Jesus didn't merely pray for unity but a unity that is rooted in the truth (John 17:17, 19). I will argue in this book that the division over justification was justified (pun intended!) since justification is integral to the gospel message we proclaim.

A brief sketch of what is to come in the ensuing chapters will assist readers in navigating this short study. We begin in chapter 1 by considering the history of the church. We aren't the first persons to consider what the Scriptures teach on justification, and thus a brief survey of how the doctrine was understood in church history is fitting. We are shaped and formed by those who have preceded us even if we are unaware of their influence, and thus traversing the historical landscape is imperative to gain a sharper profile in our own conception of the doctrine. Chapter 2 moves on to the Old Testament teaching on justification. Often people run to Paul, and to Paul only, on this matter, but such a perspective is truncated and even distorting. Sometimes Paul is portrayed as the lonely hero who trumpeted justification against all others. Even though Paul played a distinctive and formative role and presented the teaching on justification with a unique sharpness and clarity, his teaching was rooted in the Old Testament; it accorded with previous revelation.

Chapter 3 surveys what we learn from the Gospels, what we learn from Jesus of Nazareth on justification. A segment of scholarship has claimed that Paul reinvented Christianity, that his teaching was fundamentally opposed to the teaching of Jesus. Such objections have been raised particularly about justification as some have claimed that Jesus did not share Paul's understanding of justification. I will attempt to show that this objection misses the mark, that Jesus's teaching is the fountain from which Paul drinks. Paul didn't reinvent Christianity but, as one who lived in the time period after Christ's death and resurrection, faithfully unpacked the message of the Messiah. Chapter 4 brings us to Paul, and most would assent to the notion that Paul explained and expounded justification in the midst of controversy, giving the doctrine a sharper edge, a clarity that naturally emerges when debate rages.

The remainder of the New Testament is surveyed in chapter 5. Justification certainly isn't addressed with the same focus in Acts, the General Epistles, and Revelation as it is in Paul. In fact, some of these writings don't speak to the issue at all. James has been considered particularly troublesome, leading some to think that we have an outright contradiction between Paul and James. I will contend that the teaching of justification is present in this literature more than we might expect and that Paul and James should be considered allies and friends in the same gospel. Some contemporary challenges to justification by faith alone will be the subject of chapter 6. We will concentrate on the new perspective on Paul (admittedly not very new anymore!) and the apocalyptic reading of Paul.

Chapter 7 will move in a new direction as we reflect on justification and systematic theology. Here we will explore the relationship of justification to other salvific realities, such as redemption, reconciliation, adoption, sanctification, and others. I will suggest that union with Christ is the overarching category into which these other soteric realities should be placed. Can we come to any conclusions about how justification should be integrated with these doctrines? Are there any theological judgments to be made about how the various dimensions of salvation should be assessed in relation to justification? I will argue that such systematic questions aren't alien to the biblical witness but foster a greater understanding, and I will make a couple of suggestions along these lines. The book will conclude with a brief epilogue reflecting on the path traveled and what it means for us today.

1

Justification in Church History

The topic under consideration in this chapter—justification in church history—doesn't include the Old Testament and New Testament. Certainly, the scriptural witness is the most important history relative to justification, and most of this book will be devoted to the scriptural portrait of the doctrine. But in this chapter—before considering the biblical understanding—we consider briefly justification in the history of the church. It has often been said that we stand on the shoulders of those who have gone before us, and it would indeed be foolish to dive into justification without exploring what Christians in the previous centuries have said.

Some (perhaps only a few) Protestants have had the strange idea that most of what was written before our time or before the Reformation is useless or even harmful. A moment's reflection should shake us out of such a mistaken notion. Many godly and learned Christians have studied the Bible over the centuries, and their intent in studying wasn't to distort the biblical teachings so as to advance their own prejudices. Of course, they made mistakes and had blind spots, but the same is true of us. We aren't free of presuppositions and prejudices either. We don't venerate our ancestors in the faith, as if they are infallible guides to the meaning of the Scriptures and of justification in particular. Neither do we ignore them, as if they had nothing to say, as if they were all captured by alien ideologies. The Scriptures are the final authority, but the many godly believers who have walked the road of discipleship before us are also honored as our teachers.

The Early Church

Some scholars have maintained that the early church writers didn't understand Paul's teaching on justification, and thus the truth was lost in the early history of the church.[1] It seems that the situation was more complicated than this. When we actually look at the evidence, we have a number of affirmations of justification by faith and, in some cases, even of justification by faith alone.[2] The epistle 1 Clement was probably written ca. AD 96, and he clearly affirms that justification does not come from piety or works but by faith (1 Clem. 32:3–4). Similarly, the letters of Ignatius were written early in the second century. He doesn't feature the word "justification," but the concept is present, as he emphasizes the grace of Christ in his death and resurrection, finding his hope in God's mercy (*Magn.* 8:1; *Phld.* 5:1–2; 8:2; 9:2; *Smyrn.* 6:1–2; 11:1).

The most beautiful statement about justification stems from the Epistle to Diognetus 9:2–5, which was written in the second century. It is worth reproducing here in full.

1. E.g., Thomas F. Torrance, *The Doctrine of Grace in the Apostolic Fathers* (Grand Rapids, MI: Eerdmans, 1948).

2. For a defense of this view, see Brian J. Arnold, *Justification in the Second Century* (Waco, TX: Baylor University Press, 2018). See also the excellent survey from Michael Horton, *Justification*, New Studies in Dogmatics, 2 vols. (Grand Rapids, MI: Zondervan Academic, 2018), 1:39–91. This chapter draws especially on these two sources.

> But when our unrighteousness was fulfilled, and it had been made perfectly clear that its wages—punishment and death—were to be expected, then the season arrived during which God had decided to reveal at last his goodness and power (oh, the surpassing kindness and love of God!). He did not hate us, or reject us, or bear a grudge against us; instead he was patient and forbearing; in his mercy he took upon himself our sins; he himself gave up his own Son as a ransom for us, the holy one for the lawless, the guiltless for the guilty, the just for the unjust, the incorruptible for the corruptible, the immortal for the mortal. For what else but his righteousness could have covered our sins? In whom was it possible for us, the lawless and ungodly, to be justified, except in the Son of God alone? O the sweet exchange, O the incomprehensible work of God, O the unexpected blessings, that the sinfulness of many should be hidden in one righteous person, while the righteousness of one should justify many sinners![3]

The majesty and beauty of this text are striking, and we can scarcely say that no one in the early church understood justification by faith! Sinners are justified by God's grace as the Son of God took upon himself the guilt we deserved.

The Odes of Solomon were written in the second century and are relatively unknown, but they clearly teach that justification is rooted in God's kindness and grace instead of human merit (Odes Sol. 25:4), emphasizing God's gracious election (Odes Sol. 4:7; 8:13; 10:3; 12:3; 23:2–3; 41:9). It is also interesting to note that justification is understood to be forensic and not transformative (Odes Sol. 25:8, 10; 33:12), and in this respect the Odes anticipate the Reformed understanding.

3. "The Epistle to Diognetus," in *The Apostolic Fathers: Greek Texts and English Translations of Their Writings*, ed. and trans. Michael W. Holmes, 3rd ed. (Grand Rapids, MI: Baker Academic, 2007), 709, 711.

Justin Martyr engaged in a famous debate with Trypho (see *Dialogue with Trypho*) who was a Jewish opponent, and the debate between them reminds us in many respects of Paul's controversy with the Galatian false teachers. Trypho emphasized that one should be circumcised and keep the law to be saved, echoing Paul's opponents in Galatia. Justin affirms that justification is by faith, insisting that circumcision is unnecessary for salvation (*Dial.* 23.3–4; 92.2). Any works-righteousness (*Dial.* 137.1–2) is rejected since salvation comes through Jesus's work on the cross instead of performing of the law (*Dial.* 11:4–5; 137.1). Believers are righteous through Jesus's death since he died in the place of believers, taking on himself the curse believers deserve (*Dial.* 95:1–3).

Another great thinker in the early church, one who could even be described as the first to engage in biblical theology, was Irenaeus (ca. 130–202). Irenaeus doesn't work out the meaning of justification specifically, but he is famous for teaching that Jesus recapitulated human experience and that he reconciled sinners to himself in his death so that victory over sin and death is achieved in the cross of Christ.

Origen (185–254) is a rather mixed figure theologically, but he rightly discerns in the story of the thief on the cross that we are justified by faith.[4] Righteousness doesn't come, says Origen, from works of the law but is founded on our faith. At the same time, Origen emphasizes that those who exercise faith will do good works, and in this he is thoroughly biblical. Origen wasn't completely consistent, however, and also said some things that indicate a belief in merit. He anticipates the new perspective in identifying the works of the law as referring to Jewish practices. Also, Origen's notion that justification secures forgiveness only for past sins is inadequate, and it seems

4. For the view on Origen summarized here, see Horton, *Justification*, 1:54–66.

that he sees justification as a process instead of a declaration. Nick Needham has argued, however, that most of the early fathers believed justification was forensic and declarative instead of being transformative and a process.[5] Those who are Reformed recognize deficiencies in Origen, but it is also important to recognize that justification hadn't been debated and worked out thoroughly in the early church, and thus we should not be surprised by lack of precision and even some missteps along the way.

Many other testimonies could be mentioned. The fourth-century writer Theodoret of Cyrhuss comments on Ephesians 2:8: "It is not of our own accord that we have believed, . . . and even when we had come to believe, He did not require of us purity of life, but approving mere faith, God bestowed on us forgiveness of sins."[6] We see here an early and faithful commentary on Ephesians 2:8, and it is fair to say that forgiveness of sins is another way of talking about justification. Chrysostom, known as one of the greatest preachers in the early church, interpreted Ephesians 2:8 similarly. He differed from some of the Reformers, however, in his understanding of free will.[7] In any case, Chrysostom believed that one was required to obey the law perfectly to be justified, and thus human beings can't be justified by their works. Chrysostom's understanding of the works of the law matches what we see in the Reformers. Thus, justification isn't through human merit but divine grace, and the good works human beings do are a result of God's grace.

5. Nick Needham, "Justification in the Early Church Fathers," in *Justification in Perspective: Historical Developments and Contemporary Challenges*, ed. Bruce L. McCormack (Grand Rapids, MI: Baker Academic, 2006), 27–37.

6. Cited from Thomas C. Oden, *The Justification Reader* (Grand Rapids, MI: Eerdmans, 2002), 45.

7. On Chrysostom, see Oden, *The Justification Reader*, 44–45; John Chrysostom, *Homilies on Second Corinthians*, in *A Select Library of the Nicene and Post-Nicene Fathers of the Christian Church*, First Series, ed. Philip Schaff, 14 vols. (New York: The Christian Literature Company, 1889), 12:334.

Marius Victorinus wrote in the mid-fourth century, teaching that we aren't saved by our virtue nor our merits and that we can't stand in the right before God by the works of the law.[8] Salvation is by God's grace, and the good works that follow are also enabled by his grace. Hilary of Poitiers also wrote in the fourth century, affirming that justification cannot come via the law since human beings are sinners.[9] He repeatedly emphasizes that salvation is by faith. He remarks that Abraham, the thief on the cross, and the eleventh-hour workers in the vineyard (Matt. 20:1–16) are all justified by faith. Interestingly, Hilary says that justification is by faith alone: "Because faith alone justifies . . . publicans and prostitutes will be the first in the kingdom of heaven." Ambrosiaster, the name given to an unknown writer in the early church, also taught that justification was by faith alone.[10] The precision of the Reformed view is missing since he spoke about meriting a final reward. The word "merit" is unfortunate, but we may assign a meaning to the word from our post-Reformation perspective that wasn't intended by Ambrosiaster, and the latter concurred with the mainstream view in emphasizing the importance of good works.

Augustine (354–430) was a towering figure, and we can rightly say that no theologian influenced all of Christendom more than he.[11] Augustine's understanding of grace anticipated and influenced the Reformers. His doctrine of predestination should be placed within his theology of grace, and since God's electing grace brings us to faith, it follows that justification is God's gift. In Augustine's anti-Pelagian writings he regularly sounds the note that believers are saved by grace instead of

8. See D. E. H. Williams, "Justification by Faith: A Patristic Doctrine," *Journal of Ecclesiastical History* 57 (2006): 655–56.

9. For Hilary's view, including the citation here, see Williams, "Justification by Faith," 657–60.

10. See again Williams, "Justification by Faith," 662.

11. On Augustine, see Horton, *Justification*, 1:84–91.

by works, emphasizing that everything we do that is pleasing to God depends on God's gift. Every good thing in us is given graciously by God himself (1 Cor. 4:7). The works of the law aren't limited to the ceremonial law for Augustine but include the entirety of the law so that no human being may be justified before God by virtue of his goodness.

Augustine differs from the Reformers in an important respect, in that he defines the word "justify" so that it means "make righteous" instead of "declare righteous," though there are places in his writings where the declarative sense is present. Thus, for Augustine justification isn't only imputed but also inherent; it isn't a once-for-all declaration but a process, and thus justification doesn't describe a legal verdict only but also the ongoing transformation of believers. What this means is that the distinction between justification and sanctification that is well-known to those nurtured in Reformed theology doesn't represent the Augustinian perspective. In Augustine's theology sanctification and justification are two different metaphors for the progressive work of God in Christ. What stands out in his theology, however, is the efficacy of grace since God's grace grants faith and love to those whom he has elected from the foundation of the world.

Thomas Aquinas

We are skipping over a large period of time here, but the perspective of Augustine and other early writers dominated the medieval period. The next person we should consider is Thomas Aquinas (1225–74), whose thinking has influenced Roman Catholicism dramatically down to the present day.[12] The mature work of Aquinas shows that he was an Augustinian in his understanding of grace and predestination, and thus Aquinas

12. For this section, see esp. Horton, *Justification*, 1:93–129.

doesn't ground justification in the work of human beings. He rejects the idea that justification comes from obeying either the ceremonial or moral law, and thus he differs from Origen and from the Council of Trent on this score. Aquinas sees faith as a gift, but he also thinks that faith is formed by love, which was a common medieval reading of the relationship between faith and love. He says, "The movement of faith is not perfect unless it is quickened by charity; hence in the justification of the ungodly, a movement of charity is infused together with the movement of faith."[13] Endorsing the idea that faith is formed by love smuggles good works into justification, and this isn't entirely surprising since Aquinas follows Augustine in understanding justification as renovative and transformative instead of being declarative and forensic.[14] Justification is a process by which the soul is healed and changed. Faith since it is formed by love is virtuous, and thus merit plays a role in justification. Still, Aquinas assigns all merit to God's electing and predestinating grace, and thus the good human beings do comes from God himself.

Reformation

The Reformation dawned in a world where justification was understood in terms of inner renewal and transformation, following the theology of Augustine and Aquinas among others. Nevertheless, the particular conception of grace found in Augustine and Aquinas wasn't accepted by all. Gabriel Biel (ca. 1420–95) represented a common Catholic conception of the day in claiming that God helps those who do their best. In

13. See Thomas Aquinas, *Summa Theologica*, 1–2.113.4. I used the following text for Aquinas: *Summa Theologiae Prima Secundae*, 71–114, ed. John Mortensen and Enrique Alarcón, trans. Fr. Laurence Shapcote, vol. 16 of *Latin/English Edition of the Works of St. Thomas Aquinas* (Lander, WY: The Aquinas Institute for the Study of Sacred Doctrine, 2012).

14. See Aquinas, *Summa Theologica*, 1–2.113.1.

Biel's mind this understanding was still gracious since God had set up this arrangement covenantally. The emphasis was on preparing ourselves to receive the grace of God, and this was compared to putting up the sails of a ship to catch the wind or to opening the shutters of one's house to let the light stream in.[15] According to this view, human beings take the first step in their relationship with God, and the onus is on human beings to prepare themselves to receive God's grace.

A response to such teaching—a response that changed the course of history—emerged as Martin Luther (1483–1546) burst on the scene. Luther didn't use the exact words that "the church stands and falls" with respect to justification, but he clearly assents to this notion: "Because if this article [of justification] stands, the church stands; if this article collapses, the church collapses."[16] Luther counters the Augustinian tradition with respect to justification in arguing that justification is forensic—people are declared righteous, not made righteous. Such a reading represented a dramatic shift away from the majority view. Righteousness is no longer located fundamentally in the human subject. It is a legal declaration based on the death and resurrection of Jesus Christ.

Second, justification, according to Luther, should be distinguished from sanctification. Often these two were conflated and confused as if they signified the same reality. In sanctification we have a combination of faith and works, though many emphasized that all works flow from faith. Luther famously emphasized that we are justified by faith alone (German: *allein*). "We are pronounced righteous solely by faith in Christ, not by

15. For these illustrations, see Alister E. McGrath, *From the Beginnings to 1500*, vol. 1 of *Iustitia Dei: A History of the Christian Doctrine of Justification* (Cambridge: Cambridge University Press, 1986), 84–85, 90.

16. See Justin Taylor, "Luther's Saying: 'Justification is the Article by Which the Church Stands and Falls,'" *The Gospel Coalition*, August 31, 2011, https://www.thegospelcoalition.org.

the works of the Law or by love."[17] Faith alone justifies "because faith brings us the spirit gained by the merits of Christ."[18] Faith saves because it "takes hold of Christ and believes that my sin and death are damned and abolished in the sin and death of Christ."[19] Luther affirms that the life of faith isn't easy, expressing this truth powerfully. He remarks, "The words 'freedom from the wrath of God, from the Law, sin, death, etc.,' are easy to say, but to feel the greatness of the freedom and to apply its results to oneself in a struggle, in the agony of conscience, and in practice—this is more difficult than anyone can say."[20] Luther recognized that we can affirm a doctrine in our heads and find, at the same time, that it is difficult to live out in our daily lives.

In sanctification human beings are slowly transformed by the grace of God, but in justification we are declared righteous on the basis of God's work in Christ alone. As believers we are justified and at the same time sinners (Latin: *simul iustus et peccator)*. Luther doesn't deny the importance of good works, and he regularly wrote about this matter. "It is true that faith alone justifies, without works; but I am speaking about genuine faith, which after it has justified, will not go to sleep but is active through love."[21] Still, justification and sanctification should not be melded together and confused, and the fundamental character of justification must be recognized.

Along the same lines and thirdly, justification is imputed, not imparted. Believers who are united to Christ receive an alien

17. Martin Luther, *Lectures on Galatians 1535: Chapters 1–4*, ed. Jaroslav Pelikan, vol. 26 of *Luther's Works* (St. Louis: Concordia, 1964), 137.

18. Martin Luther, "Preface to the Epistle of St. Paul to the Romans," in *Martin Luther: Selections from His Writings*, ed. John Dillenberger (Garden City, NY: Doubleday, 1961), 22.

19. Luther, *Galatians 1–4*, 160.

20. Martin Luther, *Lectures on Galatians 1535: Chapters 5–6*, vol. 27 of *Luther's Works*, 5.

21. Luther, *Galatians 5–6*, 30.

righteousness.[22] The implications of this teaching are dramatic. Imputation may sound cold and legalistic, but for Luther justification becomes ours as we are married to Christ, united to him by faith. Jesus is our bridegroom, and we are his bride. We are justified because we belong to him. Justification isn't located in the human subject but is ascribed solely and completely to the grace of God.

Another interpretation of Luther's understanding of justification has surfaced today, and it is commonly labeled the Finnish view of Luther.[23] According to this reading, believers participate with Christ and are granted attributes of his divine presence. In the Finnish reading, justification is closely related to the Greek notion of *theosis,* which means believers are deified. Deification, according to this understanding, should not be read to say that believers are gods, but it emphasizes human transformation so that on this reading justification isn't forensic only. For those who accept the Finnish reading, justification and sanctification for Luther should not be distinguished since both involve moral transformation. The Finnish reading has stirred up much discussion because it represents a radically different view of Luther. It is certainly intriguing and fascinating, but it should be rejected as unconvincing.[24]

At least three reasons show the inadequacy of the Finnish interpretation of Luther. First, Luther endorsed Melanchthon's forensic and legal explanation of justification in 1531. Such an endorsement doesn't make sense if Luther believed that justification should be understood in terms of deification since

22. See Luther, "Preface to the Epistle of St. Paul to the Romans," 86–88.

23. See especially Tuomo Mannermaa, *Christ Present in Faith: Luther's View of Justification*, ed. K. Stjerna (Minneapolis: Fortress, 2005).

24. See especially Carl R. Trueman, "Is the Finnish Line a New Beginning? A Critical Assessment of the Reading of Luther Offered by the Helsinki Circle," *Westminster Theological Journal* 65 (2003): 231–44; William W. Schumacher, *Who Do I Say That You Are? Anthropology and the Theology of* Theosis *in the Finnish School of Tuomo Mannermaa* (Eugene, OR: Wipf and Stock, 2010).

Melanchthon's reading is almost the exact opposite of such an interpretation. Second, and related to the first, the Finnish interpretation concentrates on the early Luther instead of the later and mature Luther. Luther wrote and said some things early in his ministry that he qualified or even rejected as the years passed. When we study a scholar, his entire career and body of work should be considered. It makes sense, though, that the later and mature work of a scholar should be the most important. This is particularly the case with Luther who hammered out his theology in controversy, sharpening and defining his positions as time passed. Third, the credibility of the Finnish view is undermined by Luther's rejection of the teaching of Andreas Osiander (1498–1552). This isn't the place to delve into the complexities of Osiander's view, but in many respects it is quite similar to the Finnish interpretation of Luther. Luther's firm rejection of Osiander, then, is hard to understand if he endorsed the Finnish understanding. It is safe to conclude, then, that Luther's reading of justification was forensic instead of transformative and that he did not understand justification in terms of deification.

There were many luminaries in the Reformation, but in a brief survey like this we concentrate on the other great Reformer, John Calvin (1509–64), who still stands out today for his exposition and defense of the Reformed faith. Like Luther, he insisted that justification was by faith alone. Faith isn't a virtue that justifies us, but instead faith is the instrument or vehicle that unites us with Christ, confirming that we are justified by the crucified and risen one. Faith, according to Calvin, is a gift of God. We experience the sweetness of God's love and are ravished by his love, and as a consequence we put our trust in the Lord. Calvin's definition of faith is well-known. "Now we shall possess a right definition of faith if we call it a firm and certain knowledge of God's benevolence toward us, founded upon the truth of the freely given promise in Christ, both revealed to our minds and sealed upon our hearts through the Holy Spirit."[25] Justification plays a vital pastoral role since those who are justified gain assurance and confidence as they look toward the day of judgment. Some have misunderstood Calvin's view of assurance as if he believed that believers were always full of assurance and boldness, but he recognized that believers suffer ups and downs in the life of faith and that clouds could obscure the boldness we have as believers. At the end of the day faith means that we look away from ourselves and trust in Jesus Christ, that our faith grows as we consider Christ and his benefits.

Calvin also stresses that justification involves imputation. Those who put their trust in Christ are forgiven of their sins, and their righteousness is extrinsic instead of intrinsic. Justification, according to Calvin, then, is not transformative or an infusion of righteousness. Justification is a law court reality, and those who are united to Christ by faith are counted as righteous before God; they are declared righteous rather than being made righteous. Since this is the case, our justification doesn't improve or grow. We are perfect from the beginning. Calvin puts it this way, "Therefore, we explain justification simply as the acceptance with which God receives us into his favor as righteous men. And we say that it consists in the remission of sin and the imputation of Christ's righteousness."[26] According to Calvin, "We do not, therefore, contemplate him outside ourselves from afar in order that his righteousness may be imputed to us but because we put on Christ and are engrafted into his body—in short, because he deigns to make us one with him."[27]

25. John Calvin, *Institutes of the Christian Religion,* ed. John T. McNeill, trans. Ford Lewis Battles, 2 vols. (Philadelphia: Westminster, 1960), 3.2.7 (1:551).

26. Calvin, *Institutes,* 3.11.2 (1:727).

27. Calvin, *Institutes,* 3.11.11 (1:737).

Sanctification should not be confused with justification. Calvin puts this memorably: "It is therefore faith alone which justifies, and yet the faith which justifies is not alone: just as the heat alone of the sun which warms the earth, and yet in the sun it is not alone, because it is constantly conjoined with light."[28] Calvin distinguishes between justification and sanctification, but he is clear about the importance of good works, seeing them as the fruit of faith.

Roman Catholic Response: Council of Trent

It wasn't as if the church at large had come to universal agreement regarding the meaning of justification before the time of the Reformation. We saw from the earliest days of the church that there were various understandings disseminated. The Reformation understanding, however, set alarms ringing in the Catholic hierarchy. This response was formalized in the Council of Trent, which consisted of many meetings where Roman Catholic doctrine was hammered out between 1545 and 1563. Still, before the Council of Trent, there was a surprising attempt to bring a rapprochement between Roman Catholics and Protestants at the Regensburg Colloquy in 1541. Amazingly enough, the statement on justification generated significant agreement, and Calvin himself was sympathetic. Luther, on the other hand, was suspicious from the outset and felt that the statement on justification was an attempt to stitch together Protestant and Catholic views that were fundamentally contradictory. At the end of the day, the statement at Regensburg was ambiguous, and sadly the colloquy dissolved without reaching an agreement.

The controversy over justification was intense, and predictably, although unfortunately, the Council of Trent almost

28. The citation is taken from Anthony N. S. Lane, *Justification by Faith in Catholic-Protestant Dialogue: An Evangelical Assessment* (London: T&T Clark, 2002), 181.

completely repudiated the Protestant view of justification. The notion that Christians are justified by faith alone was rejected.[29] Instead, it was argued that faith and works cooperate together, and thus a progressive view of justification was endorsed.[30] Good works aren't merely the fruit of justification but were considered to be one of the causes and grounds of such.[31] All of this means that justification was understood to be inherent and infused, and thus the formula *sola fide w*as rejected. According to Trent, faith cooperates with good works and increases our justification. The relationship between faith and works enunciated at Trent indicates that justification wasn't considered to be forensic and declarative but transformative and inherent. Righteousness is imparted and infused; it is not imputed. We are not surprised, then, to find that sanctification is merged together with justification. If justification is progressive and infused, then salvation that is given to sinners when they believe can also be lost if believers cease to cooperate with God's grace. The Roman Catholic Church clarified its understanding of justification at Trent. Righteousness is inherent and not forensic, a process and not a declaration. Justification isn't by faith alone, but faith and works together constitute justification. We see, then, the sharp disjunctives that emerged over justification. For the Reformed, justification was imputed and gave assurance of salvation, but Roman Catholics rejected imputation and the notion that believers could be confident of final salvation based on Christ's imputed righteousness.

Still, Trent was over five hundred years ago, and there is a remarkable diversity in Roman Catholicism today. The conception articulated at Trent doesn't represent the view of all

29. Council of Trent, Session 6, "On Justification," January 13, 1547, https://www.papalencyclicals.net, canon 9.

30. Council of Trent, "On Justification," canon 7, 16.

31. Council of Trent, "On Justification," canon 24.

Catholics today. At the same time, we must also recognize that the *official* position of the Roman Catholic Church hasn't changed substantially since Trent, and this is seen quite clearly in the *Catechism of the Catholic Church*. For instance, the *Catechism* rightly sees that justification involves the forgiveness of sins, but it follows Trent in defining justification as "the sanctification and renewal of the inner man."[32] The influence of Augustine and his heirs is evident since justification means not only to declare righteous but also to make righteous. We read that justification "frees from the enslavement to sin" and "heals."[33] Baptism, instead of personal faith, confers the grace of justification since infants are justified when they are baptized.[34] Justification is envisioned as a cooperative project involving God and the human person[35] where both do their part. Justification and sanctification aren't distinguished since the former is described as a process that entails "the *sanctification* of his whole being."[36] The cooperation necessary in Roman Catholic theology manifests itself particularly in the role that the sacraments play in final salvation. Catholic theology recognizes that human beings can't merit God's approval in a strict sense.[37] The merit granted to human beings comes as a gracious gift from God's hand,[38] but that is not the final word since merit is also attributed "to man's collaboration."[39] The *Catechism* states, "No one can merit the initial grace which is at the origin of conversion. Moved by the Holy Spirit, we can merit for ourselves and for others all the graces needed to attain

32. *Catechism of the Catholic Church*, rev. ed. (New York: Random House, 2012), 1989; cf. 2019. The preceding numbers represent the *Catechism* paragraph numbers. So also in the following notes.
33. *Catechism of the Catholic Church*, 1990.
34. *Catechism of the Catholic Church*, 1992.
35. *Catechism of the Catholic Church*, 2002.
36. *Catechism of the Catholic Church*, 1995 (emphasis in original).
37. *Catechism of the Catholic Church*, 2007.
38. *Catechism of the Catholic Church*, 2008–2009, 2011.
39. *Catechism of the Catholic Church*, 2025.

eternal life, as well as necessary temporal goods."[40] Officially, then, Roman Catholicism has not changed its mind since Trent: justification and sanctification still portray the same state of affairs. Justification is transformative and a process, fitting with the sacramental theology of the Catholic Church.[41]

Conclusion

Our tour of history has taken us from the early church until modern Catholicism. We saw that in the early church a number of writers claimed that justification was by faith instead of works, and some even said that justification was by faith alone. At the same time, most writers also affirmed the importance of good works for salvation. Both of these themes are scarcely surprising since they are both in the Bible. The early church did not work out theologically or in a nuanced way the meaning of justification. Many conceived of justification forensically, but under the influence of Augustine the transformative understanding of justification was dominant in the Middle Ages. On the other hand, the Augustinian understanding of grace was such that many ascribed justification to God's electing grace. And yet as time passed, notions of preparing oneself to receive God's grace that emphasized the role of human choice became prominent.

The Magisterial Reformers struck out against these conceptions, articulating justification in a new and fresh way, emphasizing that justification was declarative instead of transformative, imputed instead of imparted, and extrinsic instead of intrinsic. Justification was by faith alone through grace alone to the glory of God alone. Roman Catholics at the Council of Trent and

40. *Catechism of the Catholic Church*, 2027.

41. See the important works by Gregg R. Allison, *Roman Catholic Theology and Practice: An Evangelical Assessment* (Wheaton, IL: Crossway, 2014) and *40 Questions about Roman Catholicism* (Grand Rapids, MI: Kregel Academic, 2021).

in the Catholic catechism of the twentieth century responded in turn against such Protestant understandings, affirming that human beings cooperate with God's grace in justification. They saw justification as a process where God's grace could be lost. Reformed and Lutheran orthodoxy after the Reformation consolidated and sharpened the insights of the Reformation relative to justification in the years after the dawn of the Reformation. When we look at catechisms and confessions among Catholics and orthodox Protestants, the differences between Protestants and Roman Catholics haven't changed fundamentally since the time of the Reformation, though we can find plenty of individual Protestants and Roman Catholics today who dissent from the official teaching of their church constituencies. This is not to say that new views weren't being disseminated in succeeding centuries as historical critical study began to wield its influence among biblical scholars. It isn't the purpose of this book to discuss justification in historical-critical scholarship, though some contemporary challenges to the historic Reformed position will be considered further in chapter 6.

2

The Old Testament Framework

Does the Old Testament teach justification by faith alone? We certainly don't find the explicit teaching on the doctrine that is present in the New Testament. In one sense this isn't surprising since the New Testament represents the climax of divine revelation and provides a clarity that isn't found in the Old Testament witness. We can say, however, that the Old Testament features the grace of God and that a careful reading shows that human beings are rightly related to God by faith.

The Lord called Abram who lived in Ur of the Chaldeans out of idolatry, away from the worship of other gods (Josh. 24:2–3). Abram wasn't summoned because he was particularly virtuous but on account of God's gracious purposes, because of the Lord's great mercy and love. The covenant established with Abraham was passed down and ratified with Isaac and Jacob, and neither of them, particularly Jacob, distinguished themselves with their moral integrity. Similarly, Yahweh freed Israel from Egyptian slavery, and the behavior of the people in the wilderness indicates that their redemption should not be ascribed to their moral virtue. And so it goes throughout the Old Testament from the time of the judges to the Assyrian (722 BC) and Babylonian (586 BC) exiles. Yahweh judges Israel for its sin, but he doesn't abandon them as his people, and despite their recalcitrance and disobedience he promises to make a new covenant with them (e.g., Jer. 31:31–34) and to put his law on their hearts. Israel isn't abandoned even though they have worshiped and served other gods repeatedly. Israel's relationship with the Lord is founded on his grace and mercy, not on the goodness and righteousness of the chosen people.

Two Fundamental Texts

It should prove helpful to take some samplings from the Old Testament to see how righteousness is understood, and the two texts I want to consider first are Genesis 15:6 and Habakkuk 2:4. The selection is obviously influenced by the New Testament, and there are some who would express reservations for this reason. I suggest, however, that concentrating on these two texts is not arbitrary but what all those who believe in the inspiration and authority of the Scriptures should do. To put it another way, a canonical reading of the whole Bible is imperative for Christian interpreters, for those who subscribe to the notion that the Scriptures are the word of God. Or as Christians of previous generations said, "Scripture interprets Scripture." We recognize that Genesis 15:6 and Habakkuk 2:4 are fundamental to reading the whole counsel of God, including the Old Testament, because the New Testament writers cite these texts to defend the notion of justification by faith.

Paul discusses Abraham and Genesis 15:6 in support of justification by faith in Galatians 3:6 and Romans 4:3. In fact, Paul keeps returning to Genesis 15:6 in his discussion in Romans 4, and thus he cites it in Romans 4:9 and returns to it again in Romans 4:22. We remember, of course, that James also calls upon Genesis 15:6 in James 2:23, and he seems to use it in a way that differs quite dramatically from Paul. I will return to James at a later point in this book and will argue that there isn't a disjunction between Paul and James. At this juncture the Pauline use of the text is at the forefront of our discussion. I will also consider Habakkuk 2:4, which Paul cites in Romans 1:17 and Galatians 3:11. Both of these verses are key texts where righteousness by faith is defended. Interestingly, the author of Hebrews also calls on the same text (Heb. 10:38) as he is about to launch into the great faith chapter in Hebrews 11.

My focus here isn't on the exposition of these texts in Paul and Hebrews. Instead, their citation of Genesis 15:6 and Habakkuk 2:4 sends us back to these verses in their Old Testament contexts. We want to get a taste of what is going on in both Genesis and Habakkuk, for in saying that we read canonically we are not saying that we don't read contextually. A canonical reading doesn't mean that we ignore or extinguish the voice of the texts in their historical setting. No, we read canonically *and* historically—both in terms of the whole biblical witness and in terms of the original authors. These two reading strategies should not be set against one another. Together they enrich and deepen our understanding of the biblical text. The scholarly practice of having Old Testament scholars and New Testament scholars, which makes sense given the enormity of the task in interpreting these bodies of literature, has sometimes blinded us to the unity of the Bible, to the need to read both historically and canonically.

Genesis 15:6

We begin with Genesis 15:6. In Genesis 12:1–3 Yahweh promised Abram land, offspring, and universal blessing. By

Genesis 15 some years had passed, and Abram didn't enjoy any of these promises. He didn't possess any of the land of Canaan, nor had the blessing been extended to the entire world. The latter isn't surprising, of course, since it takes time for blessing to reach the ends of the earth. Most disturbing to Abram was that he didn't have any offspring though the Lord had promised such. Genesis 15 opens with Yahweh promising Abram a great reward, but Abram, perhaps a bit cynically, has questions about the reward since he didn't have any offspring and his heir would be his servant Eliezer. Yahweh pledges to Abram that a flesh-and-blood son will be his heir, one who comes from his own body. But then the text turns to warp speed because the promise of offspring is maximized to an astonishing degree. The Lord commands Abram to go outside and to count the stars by scanning the night sky, promising Abram that his offspring will be as numerous as the stars. Perhaps the story is routine and familiar to us, but it is truly quite staggering. Abram was worried about having one son, and suddenly Yahweh tells him that he will have countless children, far beyond what he could ever ask or think. We must also recognize that Abram was quite discouraged, and thus he could have easily doubted the promise given. If the first stage of the promise hadn't even happened (having even one son that was his own), how could he possibly believe that he would have innumerable children? Still, Abram put his faith in the promises of God, and as Genesis 15:6 says, "He believed the LORD," and as a consequence Yahweh "counted it to him as righteousness."

Paul's reading of this text is on target. Abram didn't do anything here to be counted as righteous. He was completely helpless in terms of fulfilling the promise since he was an old man with a wife who was infertile. Abram was counted as righteous not because he obeyed God but because he trusted God, not because of what he achieved but because of what he believed, not because he worked for God but because he rested in God's promise. Nor would it be fitting to place the emphasis on *faith*, as if Abram was remarkably noble. Abram was righteous because he looked away from himself and his capacities and put his faith in the miraculous word of promise. Abram's faith was counted as righteousness because of the object of his faith, because his faith was in the one true God "who works for those who wait for him" (Isa. 64:4 NRSV).

An objection could be raised about the emphasis on Genesis 15:6. Didn't Abram *obey t*he Lord and leave his homeland (Gen. 12:1–4) before the events described in Genesis 15? Isn't there a sense, then, in which Abram's obedience preceded his faith? Certainly Abram obeyed the Lord in Genesis 12 by trekking to the land of promise. A canonical reading, however, provides us with an illuminating commentary on what occurred. The author of Hebrews remarks, "By faith Abraham obeyed when he was called to go out to a place that he was to receive as an inheritance" (Heb. 11:8). Abram's obedience flowed from and had its origin in his faith. We could say that faith was the root and obedience was the fruit. Does the author of Hebrews distort Genesis 12? Does he impose an alien interpretation on the narrative? Absolutely not. His construal of the account makes excellent sense. What motivated Abram to leave his homeland and family to reside in a land that he had never seen? He would not have left his homeland for a place he had never seen, and perhaps had never heard of, if he didn't rely on the promise of God, believing that he would receive what was pledged. We see here as well a close bond and tie between faith and obedience, and such a connection is forged often in the scriptural witness. Justification is by faith, even by faith alone, but that faith is never alone. True faith always changes one's life, sometimes in remarkably dramatic ways.

Habakkuk 2:4

The other text we want to think about is Habakkuk 2:4. A brief summary of Habakkuk will help us integrate the text into its contextual frame. The book opens with Habakkuk lamenting the evil and lawlessness of the nation of Judah, as he wonders how God can tolerate such wickedness. The Lord responds with the promise that he will judge his people and the means of judgment will be the terrifying military power of Babylon. But this plunges Habakkuk into another dilemma because he wonders how the Lord can use a nation that is even more wicked than Judah as the agent of judgment. The Lord doesn't answer every question, but he assures Habakkuk that Babylon will be judged as well, that its wickedness will not be forgotten or ignored, that its day of reckoning is also coming. In the midst of these declarations of judgment, we read, "The righteous shall live by his faith" (Hab. 2:4).

Before I comment further on this famous verse, we should consider the role that chapter 3 plays in Habakkuk. Here we have a psalm, which is also described as Habakkuk's prayer. We don't have space to consider the text in detail, but the imagery recalls Israel's exodus from Egypt and its triumph over enemies in days of old. The Lord's glory, power, and deliverance for his people are recounted, and the purpose is to ask God, in a day of judgment and wrath, to show mercy and renew his people again (Hab. 3:2). Just as the Lord bestowed mercy on the people in the past, Habakkuk pleads for him to do it again. The salvation and deliverance that Israel once enjoyed will be given to the nation again, but first judgment will come and devastate the people of God. Nevertheless, that's not the last word. What is true of the crops and herds will be true of Israel. The beautiful blossoms of the fig tree won't bud and flower; grapes and wine won't be harvested; food and olives will be scarce; and the flocks and herds will be insufficient. All of this paints the immediate future of Israel since they did not bear fruit but gave themselves over to evil. Still, Habakkuk trusts that the Lord will show mercy in the end and that the nation will be delivered and saved, triumphing over its foes (Hab. 3:18–19).

The prayer of Habakkuk assists us in interpreting Habakkuk 2:4. Those who are righteous believe that the Lord will ultimately save his people. Even though judgment is coming on the nation, even though there is no human reason to believe in a future for Israel since Israel has violated the law (Hab. 1:4), the righteous believe and trust that the Lord will show mercy and deliver his people as he did at the exodus, as he did in previous battles in Israel's history. Many scholars argue that the Hebrew word for faith (*emunah*) here should be translated as "faithfulness" rather than "faith," raising questions about whether Paul and the author of Hebrews appropriated this text in a way that fits the original context. I have already noted that there is an organic relationship between faith and obedience, between trusting God and living a life pleasing to him. Thus, we should not drive a hard wedge between faith and obedience. At the same time, the story of Habakkuk supports the reading of Paul and the author of Hebrews. Israel would not be rescued because of its goodness; it had failed miserably. But those who are righteous, those who belong to God, believe that the Lord will show mercy as he has in the past. He will save Israel, not because it is good but because he is so gracious.

God's Righteous Acts and His Saving Righteousness

When we think of God's righteousness in the English language, we often think first of his judgment of those who are unrighteous, of the punishment received by those who stray from his ways. And the word "righteousness" is used in the Old Testament in terms of the Lord judging Israel for abandoning the Lord and for surrendering to evil. For example, Nehemiah confesses that the Lord was righteous in punishing Israel for its wickedness (Neh. 9:33), and the author of Lamentations also acknowledges that Yahweh was in the right in sending the nation into exile (Lam. 1:18). Daniel makes the same confession as he laments the sin of Israel that prompted the Lord to send the Babylonians to displace them from their land (Dan. 9:7, 14). God's judging righteousness is apparent in Psalm 7:11:

> God is a righteous judge,
> and a God who feels indignation every day.

We could cite other texts as well (e.g., 1 Sam. 26:23; Pss. 50:6; 96:13; 99:4; 129:4), but the intuition that righteousness includes the notion that the Lord judges those who do evil is on target.

What is quite remarkable and astonishing, however, is that God's righteousness in the Old Testament often describes his saving righteousness. We see this for example in the plural use of the noun righteousness (*tsidqot*), which refers to God's saving acts for his people. For instance, Deborah and Barak, after their great victory over Israel, recount how the musicians were celebrating "the righteous triumphs of the Lord" (Judg. 5:11). God's righteous acts here don't denote his judgment but the victory and salvation he granted Israel over Sisera who was oppressing them.

Similarly, when Israel insisted on a king in 1 Samuel 12, Samuel rehearsed what God had done for the people, reminding them of the exodus under Moses and Aaron and of their victories in the past over Sisera, the Philistines, and Moab, the victories led by Gideon, Barak, Jephthah, and Samuel. These victories constituted salvation and deliverance for Israel, and Samuel characterizes them as "the righteous deeds of the LORD that he performed for you and for your fathers" (1 Sam. 12:7; cf. Isa. 45:24).

In a similar way, Micah engages in a covenant lawsuit against Israel in Micah 6, reminding Israel of the exodus and how the Lord turned the intended curse of Balaam into a blessing. He summons Israel to "know the righteous acts of the LORD" (Mic. 6:5), and they clearly represent God's saving acts for his people, his merciful goodness shown in the salvation of his people.

Or consider Psalm 103 where readers are called to bless the Lord for his goodness, for forgiving their sins, healing their diseases, redeeming them from the pit, crowning them with his faithful love and mercy, satisfying them with his goodness. He goes on to praise the Lord for his work in Moses's day, for showing mercy and compassion to Israel, particularly in removing the sin of the people. In the midst of this rehearsal, he declares,

> The LORD works righteousness
> and justice for all who are oppressed. (Ps. 103:6)

The word "righteousness" here is again the plural and in context clearly denotes God's saving acts.

Similarly, when Israel is in exile because of its sins, Daniel prays that the Lord would show mercy in harmony with all his "righteous acts," that he would save his people who were plunged into exile (Dan. 9:16). It is fascinating to observe that in every instance God's righteous acts by which he saves his people are found in contexts where Israel was sinning, where they deserved judgment and condemnation. Despite Israel's sin the Lord responds with his righteous acts, showering his mercy on his people according to his great goodness.

The plural "righteous acts" often denotes God's saving power for his people, and the singular noun "righteousness" in the Old Testament often describes his saving mercy as well. For instance, in Psalm 31:1 David prays,

> LORD, I seek refuge in you;
> let me never be disgraced.
> Save me by your righteousness. (CSB; cf. also Pss. 36:10; 40:10; 71:2)

We see the same conception in Isaiah where the Lord promises,

> I bring near my righteousness; it is not far off,
> and my salvation will not delay.
> I will put salvation in Zion,
> for Israel my glory. (Isa. 46:13; cf. also Isa. 51:4–8)

God's righteousness is manifested in saving Israel from exile in Babylon, in delivering them from an enslaving power.

It should prove helpful to examine one text a bit further. We actually begin with Paul and his claim that the gospel is God's power resulting in "salvation" (Rom. 1:16). Paul explains this salvation further (note the "for" that joins Rom. 1:17 to 1:16) as he declares that "the righteousness of God is revealed from faith to faith" (Rom. 1:17 CSB). We see that "righteousness" (*dikaiosynē*) and "salvation" (*sōtēria*) describe the good news of what God has "revealed" (*apokalyptō*) in Jesus Christ. The link between righteousness and salvation is well known, but it may not be as obvious that Paul draws on the Old Testament. The words of Psalm 98:2–3 in the Septuagint (97:2–3 LXX) reverberate in the Pauline declaration:

> The LORD has made known his salvation [*sōtērion*];
> he has revealed [*apekalypsen*] his righteousness
> [*dikaiosynēn*] in the sight of the nations.
> He has remembered his steadfast love and faithfulness
> to the house of Israel.
> All the ends of the earth have seen
> the salvation [*sōtērion*] of our God.

Three crucial words shared by the psalmist and Paul paint the background for us: "salvation," "reveal," and "righteousness." Paul picks up from the psalmist that God's righteousness is his saving righteousness and that God has unveiled that righteousness. For Paul that revelation has broken into history apocalyptically in Jesus Christ. What God has done in Christ is both new and old. The newness inaugurated in Christ's death and resurrection shatters the old world order, but it is also old since it was promised long ago. The notion that God's righteousness was saving wasn't new since it is often taught in the Old Testament, but the realization of the promise in Christ Jesus was novel.

Justification in Isaiah

We may fail to see justification in the Old Testament if we expect that it appears in a Pauline guise. What we see in the Old Testament witness, however, is that justification is dressed in other clothes, that it is expressed in different literary genres. Thus, another pathway for understanding justification opens to us in Isaiah 40–66. These chapters feature the story of Israel in exile in Babylon and the promise that the Lord will free his people and bring them back to the land.

A second exodus, a new exodus like the first when Israel was liberated from Egypt, is often promised in Isaiah (see Isa. 11:11–15; 40:3–11; 42:16; 43:2, 5–7, 16–19; 48:20–21; 49:6–11; 51:10), particularly in Isaiah 40–66. The question that arises is why Israel was in exile in the first place. In one sense the answer is easy to overlook, and in another sense it's as obvious as can be. The answer is sprinkled throughout chapters 40–66 but is expressed concisely in Isaiah 42:24:

> Who gave up Jacob to the looter,
> and Israel to the plunderers?
> Was it not the LORD, against whom we have sinned,
> in whose ways they would not walk,
> and whose law they would not obey?

Babylon wasn't the ultimate reason Israel was exiled; the Lord handed his people over since they refused to obey the Torah and rebelled against him. The reason for Israel's exile is declared clearly as well in Isaiah 50:1:

> Behold, for your iniquities you were sold,
> and for your transgressions your mother was sent away.

Indeed, the Lord was tired of Israel because of its iniquity (Isa. 43:24) so that he hid his face from his people and separated them from himself because of their sins (Isa. 59:2). Clearly, the Lord was angry with Israel because of their transgressions, raising the question whether they would ever be saved or delivered (Isa. 64:4). Israel's sins were numerous and pervasive (Isa. 59:12), a cancer that was destroying the nation's life. Actually, Isaiah 59 represents an extended reflection on the sin and transgression of God's people, and I will return to this chapter shortly. In any case, Israel sinned from the beginning, and their mediators and leaders also transgressed (Isa. 43:27). Thus the nation faced a crisis.

Since Israel was exiled because of its transgression, it needed to be delivered, rescued, redeemed, saved. Their freedom would only come through the forgiveness of sins. It is striking, therefore, that Isaiah 40 commences with the comforting promise that the days of punishment are over, that the time for mercy and forgiveness has dawned (Isa. 40:1–2). Israel will return home because of God's mercy, and he will erase (*exaleiphōn*) their sins and no longer remember them (Isa. 43:25 LXX). A synonym for erasing (*apēleipsa*) sins is used in Isaiah 44:22 LXX (though the Hebrew verb is the same in both cases), and there the sin of Israel is obscured from God's vision as the sun is hidden by the clouds. Perhaps Paul picked up this word from Isaiah when he says that the Lord erases (*exaleipsas*) our sins by nailing them to the cross (Col. 2:14). Israel's forgiveness in Isaiah means that the nation will be redeemed (*lytrōsomai*, Isa. 44:22 LXX), that it will be freed from slavery in Babylon. Ultimately, the forgiveness of Israel is secured through the servant of the Lord who "bore the sin of many" (Isa. 53:12; cf. Isa. 53:11). He "was crushed" for the "iniquities" of Israel (Isa. 53:5),

> and the Lord has laid on him
> the iniquity of us all. (Isa. 53:6)

The story of Isaiah 40–66 is this: the people were in exile because of their sin, but the Lord pledges that they will be redeemed and freed when their sin is forgiven, and ultimately their forgiveness will be accomplished by the servant of the Lord. Remarkably, this deliverance of Israel, described as we have already seen in terms of forgiveness of sins and redemption, is also designated as God's righteousness. Yes, righteousness may stand for God's judgment, but Isaiah uses the term quite regularly for God's saving righteousness. We see this clearly in Isaiah 45:8:

> Shower, O heavens, from above,
> and let the clouds rain down righteousness;

let the earth open, that salvation and righteousness may
bear fruit;
let the earth cause them both to sprout;
I the LORD have created it.

God's righteousness here is clearly his saving righteousness, a righteousness that will be displayed when Israel returns from Babylonian bondage. As Isaiah 46:13 declares, when God's "righteousness" arrives, so too does "salvation." We see the same theme in Isaiah 51:5–8. God's "righteousness" signals his "salvation" for his people, the deliverance that will be theirs because the Lord has forgiven their sins (cf. Isa. 56:1; 61:10–11; 62:1–2; 63:1).

It is fitting to conclude this brief side stop at Isaiah by considering Isaiah 59 since it pulls together several themes we have been thinking about. The chapter begins by affirming that Israel's plight can't be ascribed to the Lord's weakness but to Israel's sin. Israel is separated from God and doesn't see his face and experience his favor because of its iniquity (Isa. 59:1–2). The sin of the nation is rehearsed: murder, deception, lying, unjust lawsuits, violence, and false claims to holiness. They have repeatedly violated the covenant stipulations and thus are facing the curses of the covenant (see Lev. 26; Deut. 27–28). The people don't know peace but inflict havoc and misery wherever they go since they don't fear God. Paul calls on Isaiah 59 in Romans 3:15–18 as he sketches in the universality of sin, the fundamental problem with all people everywhere. The justice and righteousness Israel hoped for eludes them because of their sin so that they are plunged into darkness and gloom instead of enjoying the light of life. Israel is like a blind person groping in the dark. Salvation and justice are not their portion because of their sin, their transgressions, their apostasy.

The picture is bleak in the extreme, but the text turns a corner. The Lord saw that deliverance would not come from human beings, and thus

> his own arm brought him salvation,
>   and his righteousness upheld him.
> He put on righteousness as a breastplate,
>   and a helmet of salvation on his head. (Isa. 59:16–17)

The subsequent verses demonstrate that God's righteousness includes his wrath and judgment against those who indulge in evil. But there is also a promise that some will fear the Lord, the Spirit will turn their hearts toward home, and redemption will come again to Israel. Israel deserves God's judging righteousness, but that isn't the only word, nor is it the last word. A day is coming when God's saving righteousness will dawn, when the promises of life and light will become a reality, when the sins of Israel will be forgiven. They will return from exile, and it is clear from the New Testament and Isaiah 53 that Israel's sins are forgiven, not because of their own virtue but because of the servant of the Lord, because he takes on himself the punishment Israel deserved. So Isaiah's message is one of justification, of God's saving righteousness to the undeserving, a saving righteousness that is theirs through the atoning death of the servant of the Lord. This is Isaiah's way of saying that the ungodly are justified by God's grace (Rom. 4:5).

Righteousness in Job

The book of Job doesn't explicitly teach the justification of the ungodly, but I want to open a brief window onto the book since Job often talks about righteousness. In the midst of his suffering and anguish, Job asks for a trial before God, confident that if a fair trial were conducted, he would be vindicated. Even though

Job is sure that his punishment can't be ascribed to sin, he complains that he can't get a court date before God since God is so powerful and mighty that no one can compel him to come to court (Job 9:14–22). In fact, God, according to Job, unjustly condemns him, even though Job stands in the right. Job regularly returns to his desire to go to court with God so that he can argue his case before him (Job 13:3), indicting his friends for using specious arguments to defend God (Job 13:4–12). If God is in the right, he doesn't need terrible arguments from friends to support him! Job is convinced that he would be acquitted if a trial were held, but God's power terrifies him and hinders him from being able to make his plea (Job 13:18–24). God's majesty, greatness, and power make a fair trial almost impossible since he overwhelms Job with his presence so that Job can't say what he wants to say. On another occasion Job says that he wants to argue his legal case before God, and he is sure that if he could make the case that God would acquit him of the charges (Job 23:2–7). Job isn't completely consistent in his speeches, but we understand since he speaks from the pain, terror, and anguish of his heart. His friends frustrate him and are treacherous. Job remains convinced, despite the arguments of his friends, that he is in the right and concludes that God has wronged him (Job 27:2–6). His last speech in Job 31 captures in a virtuoso performance his defense, as he presents before the world and God why his behavior did not warrant the suffering he experienced.

Several texts in Job show that the issue is his righteousness before God. Job asks the question that burns in his heart:

> Truly, I know that it is so:
> But how can a man be in the right before God?
> (Job 9:2)

Zophar is persuaded that Job is guilty:

> Should this abundance of words go unanswered
> and such a talker be acquitted? (Job 11:2 CSB)

Job, on the other hand, counters the narrative of his friends:

> Now then, I have prepared my case;
> I know that I am right (Job 13:18 CSB)

Despite being battered with criticism, Job contends to the end:

> I hold fast my righteousness and will not let it go;
> my heart does not reproach me for any of my days.
> (Job 27:6)

When all the speeches are finished, Elihu reproaches Job:

> Job has declared, "I am righteous,
> yet God has deprived me of justice." (Job 34:5 CSB)

The Lord agrees with Elihu's charge:

> Would you really challenge my justice?
> Would you declare me guilty to justify yourself?
> (Job 40:8 CSB)

Job correctly claims that he is in the right in that he isn't suffering because of his sin, but he has gone too far in saying that God is unjust.

I am not attempting here to offer an interpretation of the book of Job. The point of this broad sweep is that a central concern in the book is justification. No, Job doesn't talk about the justification of the ungodly in the same way as Paul. Still, he and his friends argue about whether Job would be vindicated in trial in the divine court. Job's desperation and insistence of his righteousness reaches the stage where he says that he is in the right and God is in the wrong! He takes a step too far, but his claim demonstrates that the book of Job isn't simply about suffering but about the righteousness of the sufferer, and the book as a whole teaches us that Job isn't suffering because of his personal sin.

Conclusion

We have seen in this chapter that God's saving righteousness isn't a minor theme in the Old Testament. Two central texts (Gen. 15:6 and Hab. 2:4) confirm that those who stand in the right before God do so by faith. In the Old Testament God's righteousness has different meanings according to the context. In some texts God's righteousness is his judging righteousness, as he justly punishes those in sin. In addition, we saw that the noun "righteousness" in both the singular and the plural often designates God's saving righteousness, the righteousness by which he delivers his people from their enemies and from their sin.

Isaiah 40–66 is particularly interesting. The people of Israel had been exiled to Babylon because of their sin, but the Lord promised that he would forgive their sins, and ultimately this forgiveness would be secured by the suffering of the servant of the Lord who would bear the sins of his people. The return from exile, the forgiveness of sins pledged to Israel, is described as the Lord's righteousness, his saving righteousness, his merciful deliverance of his people.

Finally, we saw in Job that a central question was whether Job would be counted as right before the divine judge. In one way, the entire book is about Job's righteousness. The New Testament and Pauline emphasis on justification and righteousness is not a Pauline invention; it is a central concern of the Old Testament. And no wonder, for whether we stand in the right before the divine Judge is surely one of the most important questions in our lives.

3

Jesus and Justification

One of the themes of this book (though it is not the only theme!) is that justification through faith alone by grace alone is not restricted to Paul, nor did it begin with Paul. We saw in the last chapter that justification by faith is rooted and grounded in the Old Testament, and in this chapter we will explore justification in the teaching of Jesus. In speaking of justification, I am not thinking of the word "justification" but the concept. When we think of justification conceptually instead of just verbally, we see that Jesus taught justification in his own idiom and his own way before Paul ever came on the scene. It has long been recognized that a word-study approach is reductionistic, and thus we need to include texts and accounts that have the concept of justification, even if the term itself is absent. To put it another way: Paul got his teaching of justification from Jesus himself. In this chapter I will take some snapshots of Jesus's teaching on this matter, and readers should know that I am just scratching the surface, gliding over the waves quickly. Much more could be said.

Welcoming Tax Collectors and Sinners

We begin with Jesus's table fellowship with tax collectors and sinners (Matt. 9:10–13; 11:19; 21:31–32; Mark 2:15–17; Luke 5:30–32; 7:29, 34; 15:2; 19:1–10). Tax collectors were despised for two reasons. First, they collaborated with the hated Romans who were an alien power ruling over Israel, and thus tax collectors were considered to be unpatriotic. Second, tax collectors often skimmed money off the top, charging more than was warranted to enrich themselves. Many in Israel believed that living righteously mandated avoiding sinners, keeping away from them to ensure one's own purity.

Jesus doesn't deny that tax collectors and sinners have wandered from God's way, nor does he teach that they can stay as they are, as if they could enjoy fellowship with Jesus even if they don't repent from their sins. Yet he doesn't shun them but mixes with them, even eating at table with them. In many ways having a meal with others is not different today, communicating love, friendship, conviviality, and joy. Jesus reaches out to those who have strayed from God, inviting them to return, offering them forgiveness and a new start. The social elite and even ordinary people had turned their back on this class of people, but Jesus differs in calling them to be disciples and inviting them to repent. He has come as the great physician to heal those who are sick (Matt. 9:12). Jesus came particularly to summon sinners to repentance and faith (Matt. 9:13)—people like Matthew who made his living as a tax collector before he met Jesus (Matt. 9:9). He doesn't abandon those who have rebelled and strayed but calls them to repentance. Eating together with tax collectors and sinners enacts the truth that they are justified by faith instead of by works. They are not right with God because of their goodness but because of the grace of God that is poured out in the ministry of Jesus.

The story of Zacchaeus (Luke 19:1–10), a chief tax collector, illustrates the truth that we are considering. Many people in Israel were disgusted that Jesus agreed to enter the home of such a notorious sinner and traitor. The point of the story is enunciated in Luke 19:10, "For the Son of Man came to seek and to save the lost." Zacchaeus was lost, but there was hope; there was forgiveness; there was a new beginning for him. We could say that the unrighteous was now righteous through the mercy of Christ. We need to remember that these stories of Jesus sitting at table and welcoming tax collectors and sinners are preserved because they were characteristic of his ministry, illustrating the love of God and the forgiveness offered to all who would repent and believe.

The Parable of the Prodigal Son

The story of the prodigal son (really the story of the two lost sons!) accords with the truth that God's forgiveness is free and unearned (Luke 15:11–32). Jesus told this parable after the religious leaders complained that he was welcoming sinners and eating with them (Luke 15:1–2). The prodigal son, then, represents the tax collectors and sinners, while the older son stands for the Pharisees and religious leaders. The tale of the prodigal son is well known. He demands his part of the inheritance, moves far away from his father, ruins his own life by indulging his pleasures, and becomes a hired hand who is forced to feed pigs, which were unclean animals. Things were so dire, and he was so famished, that he wished he could eat the food the pigs were gorging themselves on. But he came to himself, realizing that there was hope if he returned to his father as long as he acknowledged his fault and was willing to live as one of his father's servants. The father, however, was filled with mercy and compassion, running to meet his son, even though running was not considered to be dignified for an older man. The son acknowledges his sin and unworthiness to belong to the family, showing that Jesus did not welcome tax collectors and sinners into fellowship and a right relationship with himself apart from repentance. Repentance should be understood as a relational act—a turning to God himself and a turning away from sin. After the son returned and repented, no more is said about his sin. Instead, he is arrayed with a robe, a ring, and shoes. The fattened calf is slaughtered and the party begins with music and dancing.

The parable captures the picture of justification by grace beautifully; the prodigal didn't earn acceptance with the father by living as a respectable and godly son. He had failed miserably and, it seemed, irretrievably. But Jesus reveals the mercy and grace of God, showing that there is a way back for those who have sinned egregiously and for all those who have wandered from God. Those who admit their need, those who acknowledge their unworthiness, those who reach out an empty hand for help are forgiven. They are not chastised: they are welcomed with joy, with a party, with celebration.

The Parable of the Pharisee and the Tax Collector

Another famous parable that illustrates the justification of sinners is the parable of the Pharisee and tax collector (Luke 18:9–14). Before the parable begins, Luke tells us what the parable is about, and as readers we welcome explicit hermeneutical help. Jesus "also told this parable to some who trusted in themselves that they were righteous, and treated others with contempt" (Luke 18:9). Often, we are given scant or no interpretive help in understanding a parable, but in this case Luke tells us what the parable is about before it begins! As readers, then, we should pay particular attention to the Lukan comment. The parable isn't directed against all; it isn't addressed to those who are deeply conscious of their failings and sins. It is directed to those who are self-sufficient, to those who think they are righteous, convinced that they are better than others.

Both the Pharisee and the tax collector approach the temple for prayer (Luke 18:10), and this makes perfect sense since the Lord specially dwells in the temple. Solomon emphasized in his prayer (see 1 Kings 8) when the temple was built that those who pray toward the temple and ask for forgiveness will be cleansed. We should also note the posture of the two men. The Greek text could be read in various ways, but the most likely reading is that the Pharisee stands by himself, while the tax collector stands far away (Luke 18:11, 13). The Lukan interpretive comment in 18:9 helps us understand what is going on. The Pharisee stands by himself because he thinks he is better than others. He doesn't want to be corrupted and defiled by the unclean and by the sinful. He wants to keep a safe distance from those who are wicked, especially the tax collector. In contrast, the tax collector, like the prodigal son, stands far away because he feels unworthy, knowing the depth of his sin.

The Pharisee gives thanks to God as he evaluates himself, concluding that he is better than others since he has avoided extortion, unrighteousness, and adultery. He is grateful that he isn't like other people, particularly the tax collector who is in his field of vision. The Pharisee has abstained from sin, but he has done even more than that; he has practiced righteousness, fasting twice a week and tithing more than is required. Luke has already told us that the parable is for those who think they are righteous and who despise others. The Pharisee's prayer exhibits his pride, arrogance, and elitism—his confidence that he is far above ordinary mortals.

Just as Luke introduced the parable with an authorial comment, so too Jesus concludes the parable with a pithy and memorable saying (Luke 18:14): "I tell you, this man went down to his house justified, rather than the other. For everyone who exalts himself will be humbled, but the one who humbles himself will be exalted." The lesson we should draw from the Pharisee is that he exalted himself, that he elevated himself above his peers, and that he congratulated himself for his virtue. But those who esteem and elevate themselves will be humbled. The two frames (18:9 and 18:14) of the parable play a decisive role in interpreting its meaning.

Some have claimed that the Pharisee believed that his triumph over sin and the virtues present in his life should be attributed to God's grace since he *thanked God*. That is a most interesting interpretation, but it is almost certainly wrong. The Pharisee's thanksgiving should not be taken seriously as if it reflected his heart, as if he was truly praising God for the change in his life, as if he was truly giving God the glory for the change in his life. No indeed. Luke informs us from the outset that he trusted himself (Luke 18:9). His trust and dependence weren't on the Lord but rested on his own virtue. The comment from Jesus in Luke 18:14 confirms the same point. The Pharisee didn't authentically thank God for his goodness but was exalting himself. In other words, he knew the right words to say in the prayer, but he wasn't truly thanking the Lord. In fact, he was praising and exalting himself and trusting himself! The thanks offered to God should not be read as if he was truly crediting the Lord for his changed life. Those who are truly grateful to the Lord don't vaunt themselves above others, nor do they place their trust in themselves. In truth, the Pharisee fits with what the apostle Paul says: he "worshiped and served the creature rather than the Creator" (Rom. 1:25).

The tax collector contrasts dramatically with the Pharisee. We already saw that he stands far away because of his humility, and his humility is also attested by not even lifting his eyes (Luke 18:13). Not lifting the eyes echoes Psalm 131:1:

> O Lord, my heart is not lifted up;
> my eyes are not raised too high.

By way of contrast, "how lofty are" the "eyes" of the proud; "how high their eyelids lift" (Prov. 30:13). Moreover, the tax collector beats his breast, which physically expresses grief and intense anguish (see Isa. 32:12; Nah. 2:7; Luke 23:48). He doesn't parade his virtues before God, nor does he extol himself for the vices he has refrained from indulging in. He simply pleads, "God, be merciful to me, a sinner" (Luke 18:13). The commentary in Luke 18:14 indicates that he humbled himself, and thus he would be exalted. He didn't trust in his own righteousness (Luke 18:9) but looked away from himself to God for the forgiveness of his sins.

Remarkably, Jesus says that the tax collector—who didn't trust in his own righteousness but humbled himself—was justified (*dedikiaōmenos*) rather than the Pharisee. We find clearly here the "Pauline" teaching of justification in the words of Jesus, which tells us that Jesus taught the justification of the ungodly before Paul came along. We also see from this parable that works-righteousness or legalism was an actual problem in Second Temple Judaism. Clearly, the Pharisee thought his works merited God's favor; it is hard to escape that conclusion in reading the parable. The Pharisee thought his works would justify or vindicate him, but the vindication of the tax collector illustrates the justification of the ungodly (Rom. 4:5). Some scholars claim that virtually no one believed in works-righteousness in Judaism, but if that is true it is difficult to understand why Jesus tells this parable since Jesus wasn't in the habit of telling stories that have nothing to do with everyday life. Actually, if we think about it, we realize that self-justification functions as a powerful motive in all of our lives. We want to say to the world and to God that we should be praised for what we have done. We don't want to humble ourselves and beg for mercy. We want to exalt ourselves and to be respected like the Pharisee.

The Gift of Righteousness and Forgiveness

The parable of the Pharisee and tax collector uses the verb "justify," but we don't need the word "justification" to see that Jesus regularly lived out and taught the truth that our righteousness isn't ultimately in ourselves but is a gift granted to us by faith. Jesus begins the Sermon on the Mount by declaring, "Blessed are the poor in spirit, for theirs is the kingdom of heaven" (Matt. 5:3). The kingdom belongs to those who are impoverished spiritually, to those who see their utter emptiness, their moral vacuity. Of course, all people are in this state, but Jesus speaks of those who *recognize* their weakness, nakedness, and poverty, of those who realize that spiritual riches only come from God. Thus, we "hunger and thirst for righteousness" (Matt. 5:6) since it doesn't reside in ourselves. Such righteousness must be granted to us, bestowed graciously on us by the God and Father of our Lord Jesus Christ.

Justification and forgiveness of sins are closely related. Matthew signals at the outset that Jesus came to "save his people from their sins" (Matt. 1:21). Forgiveness is secured through the shedding of his blood (Matt. 26:28) since he dies as "a ransom for many" (Matt. 20:28). In the account of the paralytic, four men lower the paralyzed man down through the roof at Jesus's feet, showing their determination to see him healed (Mark 2:1–12). Jesus astonished all by declaring the man was forgiven of his sins. The narrative concentrates on Jesus's authority as the Son of Man to make such a pronouncement, but my purpose here is to reflect briefly on what is pronounced. Obviously, the man needed forgiveness, or Jesus's words would be meaningless. Furthermore, it is quite clear that the man and his friends came to Jesus with faith that he could heal (Mark 2:5). Still, the most natural way to read the account is that the forgiveness granted was free and undeserved, an astonishing gift to one burdened with sins. Since Jesus also healed the paralytic, the words of Psalm 103:3 echo in the story: God "forgives all your iniquity" and "heals all your diseases." The next verse (Ps. 103:4) praises the Lord for his faithful love and mercy, intimating that forgiveness of sins is all of grace.

The Sinful Woman

Perhaps the most remarkable story about forgiveness of sins is Jesus's encounter with the sinful woman in Luke 7:36–50. Simon the Pharisee invited Jesus for a meal, but a woman well known for her sin, which was probably sexual sin since it was noised about, arrived at the party. Since it was a formal meal, those eating were likely reclining with their heads at the table and their feet stretched behind them, which helps explain what happened next. The woman entered weeping. Her tears fell on Jesus's feet, and she proceeded to wipe them dry with her hair. Then she kissed his feet and anointed them with perfume. Simon was scandalized, concluding that if Jesus were a prophet he would not allow a sinful woman like this to touch him. Jesus immediately proved to Simon that he was a prophet since he read his mind. Jesus posed a seemingly typical rabbinic question to Simon asking who would love a creditor more—one forgiven a small debt or one forgiven a gargantuan amount. The answer is obvious: the one forgiven a large debt will love more. Jesus surprised Simon by applying his parable to the sinful woman. She demonstrated her love for Jesus by giving him the greeting

Simon failed to give when Jesus arrived. Simon didn't give Jesus water to cleanse his feet, but she cleaned his feet with her tears and hair. Simon didn't give Jesus a kiss of greeting, but she kissed his feet. Simon didn't anoint Jesus's head with oil, but she anointed his feet with perfume. Thus, Jesus declares that she was forgiven of her sins on account of her love, declaring that those who are forgiven much love much.

Some have read Jesus to say that the woman is forgiven on the basis of her love. But this reading should be rejected as alien to the story. The whole point of the parable Jesus told Simon is that those who are forgiven much respond in love. Love doesn't merit forgiveness—forgiveness comes first, giving birth to love and gratefulness. Hence, Jesus declares to the woman, "Your sins are forgiven" (Luke 7:48). We see here another picture of the justification of the ungodly. The sinful woman burdened with shame and guilt is told that her past life isn't taken into account, that her debt no longer stands against her, that a new life has begun. The story ends with another declaration from Jesus addressed to the woman: "Your faith has saved you; go in peace" (Luke 7:50). This is very Pauline, or we should say that Paul is very much influenced by Jesus! The woman didn't receive forgiveness by working but by believing, by trusting, by relying on the word of promise. Because she is forgiven, she can leave at peace, which reminds us of Romans 5:1, that those who are justified by faith have peace with God. We can't prove it, but I think Paul got that notion from this story. Luke and Paul traveled together, and it is hard to believe that they didn't talk about what Jesus said and did. Those who trust in God's free forgiveness and receive it enjoy peace with God and assurance of faith.

The words "your faith has saved you" remind us of Ephesians 2:8: "For by grace you have been saved through faith.

And this is not your own doing; it is the gift of God." I suggest, then, that Jesus influenced Paul, that the Pauline teaching on faith saving us harkens back to Jesus himself. Actually, the expression "your faith has saved you" (*hē pistis sou sesōken se*) occurs three other times in Luke (Luke 8:48; 17:19; 18:42). Most translations rightly render this phrase "your faith has made you well" since in these latter cases the person is healed of a malady. We have a prime example here of how English translations can't do everything because rendering the phrase as "your faith has saved you" is also a faithful rendering. To put it another way, in every case we see both a physical and a spiritual healing. Let's consider further what it means to say that "your faith has saved you."

Your Faith Has Saved You

Three texts where Jesus declares, "Your faith has saved you," will be considered briefly. In the first, when a large crowd was jostling him, a woman who suffered from a hemorrhage for twelve years approached Jesus, touching the tassel on his robe (Luke 8:43–48). She was healed instantly but intended to steal away without informing others about what had happened. Jesus, however, knowing what had happened, insisted that someone had touched him, though Peter remonstrated that no person could be singled out for touching Jesus since the crowd surrounded him. Still, Jesus, knowing that this particular touch brought healing, solicited the woman to declare all that had occurred. After she revealed all, Jesus declared, "Your faith has saved you. Go in peace" (Luke 8:48 CSB). Jesus's words match exactly what he said to the sinful woman (Luke 7:50). Jesus's words surely mean that she has been healed, that she is now physically whole. We saw, however, in the citation of Psalm 103:3 above that healing and forgiveness are closely conjoined.

It is likely, then, that her faith saving her also speaks to her spiritual state, to her relation to God, to her being saved from sin and its consequences.

We also read about the ten lepers who implored Jesus to show them mercy and were cleansed of their leprosy (Luke 17:11–19). They were healed while making their way to the priests (cf. Lev. 13–14) per Jesus's instructions. Still only one returned to Jesus to give thanks and glory to God for his cleansing, and the one who returned stands out since he was a Samaritan. It seems that the rest took the healing for granted and weren't deeply grateful. Jesus remarked on the fact that only the Samaritan returned to give thanks, and he concluded with the words, "Your faith has saved you" (Luke 17:19 CSB). These final words were addressed solely to the returning Samaritan. Yes, all ten were healed, all ten were made well, but only the Samaritan heard the words, "Your faith has saved you." This suggests that the Samaritan was cleansed in a deeper and more profound way than the other nine. All were healed physically, including the Samaritan, but the Samaritan had been cleansed both physically and spiritually. His faith saved him not only from disease but also from sin.

The last story to be considered is the healing of the blind man near Jericho (Luke 18:35–43). As Jesus passed by, the blind man hailed him as the "Son of David," asking Jesus to show him mercy (Luke 18:38–39). The man asked that his sight be restored, and Jesus instantly and miraculously restored his sight. Jesus declared, "Your faith has saved you" (Luke 18:42 CSB). Certainly, his faith made him well physically, but as we have seen previously there is probably a double meaning in the phrase. After all, the man didn't only ask Jesus to shower him with mercy, he also identified him as the Son of David, meaning in the framework of Luke's Gospel that he recognized Jesus as the Messiah. Furthermore, not only did he receive healing but after his healing he followed Jesus. Following Jesus is what disciples do, and thus the once-blind man is painted as a disciple of Jesus. And we shouldn't stop there since he followed Jesus as Jesus went to Jerusalem to die. Jesus said that disciples must take up their cross and follow him (Luke 9:23), and we have every indication that the blind man was following in Jesus's steps as Jesus goes to the cross. Historically, of course, the blind man didn't know that Jesus was going to the cross, but it is likely that Luke sees theological significance in the blind man following Jesus to Jerusalem. In any case, the blind man wasn't healed or saved because of his virtue. Jesus showed him mercy as he reached out in faith, and that is the message of justification in a story, in a historical narrative. It may not have every element of justification as it is explicated theologically, but the fundamental reality is present.

All three of these texts emphasize that faith saves, and I suggest again that Paul's emphasis on faith—yes, faith alone—was mediated to him by the teaching of Jesus. Paul stresses repeatedly, as we shall see, that salvation and justification are by faith, but Jesus preceded Paul in enunciating this truth, as those who were made whole both spiritually and physically are told that their faith, their trust, their reliance on God, accounted for the newness that characterized their lives.

Gospel of John

John in his Gospel doesn't use the language of justification. The idiom, the metaphors, the images differ, but the reality is the same. It is striking, for instance, that John uses the verb "believe" (*pisteuō*) ninety-eight times and the word "life" (*zōē*) thirty-six times, indicating that these are central themes. Indeed, the two are often linked together in John (e.g., John 3:15, 16,

36; 5:24; 6:35, 40, 47; 11:25; 20:31). Actually, these two words appear in John 20:31, a massively important verse since it communicates the purpose of the Gospel: "These are written so that you may believe that Jesus is the Christ, the Son of God, and that by believing you may have life in his name." The most famous verse in the Gospel and perhaps in the entire Bible also joins these two themes: "For God so loved the world, that he gave his only Son, that whoever believes in him should not perish but have eternal life" (John 3:16).

Where Paul speaks of "justification," John speaks of "life," but they both agree that life is obtained through believing. Actually, there is a closer connection between life and justification in Paul than is sometimes recognized. For instance, in Galatians 3:11 Paul declares that "no one is justified before God by the law," but he supports this claim by citing Habakkuk 2:4, "The righteous shall live by faith." It seems here that the verbs justify (*dikaioutai*) and live (*zēsetai*), even though they are not synonyms, are two alternate ways of describing what we can call salvation. Paul cites the same verse from Habakkuk 2:4 in Romans 1:17 where he introduces God's righteousness in verses that are often described as the theme of the letter (Rom. 1:16–17). All of this is to say that we should not drive too sharp of a wedge between Paul and John since they both speak of life being obtained through believing.

The most important connection isn't between justification and life when we think about John and Paul. Instead, the vital place where they meet is the importance of believing. John 6:22–59, typically designated as the bread of life discourse, functions as an example where the emphasis on trust or belief is quite striking. Jesus was in the midst of a back-and-forth debate with a crowd. They were entranced that he was able to feed five thousand people, but they also had doubts about his identity. Jesus confronted the priority they put on physical sustenance, saying that they must not "work for the food that perishes, but for the food that endures to eternal life" (John 6:27). This provoked the crowd to ask what they would have to do to perform God's works (John 6:28). Jesus replied, "This is the work of God, that you believe in him whom he has sent" (John 6:29). Jesus didn't summon the crowd to work for God but to believe in Jesus as the bread of God, to rest in his death as that which gives "life to the world" (John 6:33; cf. 6:51). What it means to eat his flesh and to drink his blood (John 6:51–58) is to trust in his torn and broken flesh that grants life. Those who believe enjoy eternal life and will never face judgment on the last day (John 5:24; 6:47).

We could examine many other texts where John emphasizes the importance of believing, but we see clearly in John 6 that Jesus calls those who want to *work* for him to *believe* in him. The Gospel of John in its own idiom and manner of speaking emphasizes that life comes from believing and trusting in Jesus as the Son of God. There is a passivity and receptiveness to believing since we receive life from another. On the other hand, any reference to passivity could be misunderstood, for in another sense believing is living and active. And yet believing should be distinguished from working; those who believe *receive* (*elabon*) him (John 1:12; cf. 17:8). They welcome and accept and rest in who Jesus is and what he has done.

Conclusion

As we have peeked into the Gospels, we have seen that even though the word "justification" isn't common, the reality and conception is present. Paul unpacks the meaning of justification in his epistles, but the same truth is communicated in the Gospels with stories and parables that are unforgettable in their power and beauty: the calling of Matthew and Zacchaeus as tax collectors; the parable of the prodigal son and the parable of the Pharisee and tax collector; and the story of the sinful woman who showed up as the surprise guest at Simon the Pharisee's dinner. Jesus welcomed tax collectors and sinners, inviting all who had made a wreck of their lives and all who had rebelled against God to come to him for life and forgiveness. He declared that those who believed are forgiven. One doesn't have to measure up to a certain standard of goodness to belong to Jesus. Instead, people are called to believe, to repent, and to put their trust in him. He proclaimed that faith saves, that trust in him gives hope and a new relationship with God.

The Gospel of John travels along the same arteries, emphasizing that those who believe, those who receive, those who trust—and not those who work—enjoy eternal life. The Lord doesn't call on people to work for him but to believe in him and to rest in his kind and merciful love. When we come to Paul we should recognize his dependence on the teaching of Jesus. Paul's teaching on justification didn't originate from himself; he was a faithful disciple of Jesus.

4

Justification of the Ungodly in Paul

Importance of Justification in Paul's Thought

It might surprise some to learn that the prominence of justification in Paul's theology has been the subject of debate. Some in the Reformation tradition have understood justification to be the center of Paul's theology, but others have pushed back against this notion—some even suggesting that justification plays a relatively minor role in Paul's thought. At the beginning of the twentieth century, Albert Schweitzer famously said that justification is just "a subsidiary crater" in Paul's thought and that union with Christ is central.[1] William Wrede went even further and said that justification doesn't even need to be included in explaining Paul's theology since he only mentions it when debating with adversaries.[2] It is a mistake to put justification at the center of Paul's thought, but it shouldn't be

1. Albert Schweitzer, *The Mysticism of Paul the Apostle* (New York: H. Holt, 1931), 225.

2. William Wrede, *Paul* (Lexington, KY: American Theological Library Association, 1962), 122–23.

minimized either. Michael Allen rightly says that the doctrine is very important since it is linked indissolubly with central Christian teachings: Christ's death and resurrection, salvation, grace, atonement, and God's glory.[3] Also, we should reject the idea that justification isn't important since it is prominent in letters where Paul argues with opponents. After all, we typically fight over what we think is important.[4]

It is also off the mark to say that justification only surfaces in political battles. In 1 Corinthians 1:30 Paul declares that Christ is our "righteousness and sanctification and redemption," and there is no evidence that justification was debated in the first letter to the Corinthians. In this text when Paul thinks of the salvation enjoyed by the Corinthians, he lists justification first. Similarly, Paul reminds the Corinthians when they are slipping into sin, "But you were washed, you were sanctified, you were justified in the name of the Lord Jesus Christ and by the Spirit of our God" (1 Cor. 6:11). What is interesting here is that the issue before the Corinthians is their lifestyle, their deviation from what is good and right and true. Still, Paul includes justification as one of the great benefits believers enjoy, and the truth and reality of justification should motivate Christians to live in a way the pleases God. Or consider 2 Corinthians 5:21: "For our sake he made him to be sin who knew no sin, so that in him we might become the righteousness of God." I will return to this verse later, but here I note that in a discussion of reconciliation Paul turns to justification to unpack what God has done in Christ. Similarly, as Paul explains his new covenant ministry, he contrasts "the ministry of condemnation" to "the

3. R. Michael Allen, *Justification and the Gospel: Understanding the Context and Controversies* (Grand Rapids, MI: Baker Academic, 2013), 3–19.

4. Mark A. Seifrid, *Christ, Our Righteousness: Paul's Theology of Justification*, New Studies in Biblical Theology 9 (Downers Grove, IL: IVP Academic 2000), 77–93, rightly emphasizes the importance of justification in Paul's theology.

ministry of righteousness" (2 Cor. 3:9), and the importance of justification is clear since it is linked to covenant.

Sometimes people say that the Pastoral Epistles move away from the Pauline gospel, but in Titus 3:5–7 justification is closely related to regeneration, eternal life, the gift of the Spirit, and the believer's inheritance:

> [God] saved us, not because of works done by us in righteousness, but according to his own mercy, by the washing of regeneration and renewal of the Holy Spirit, whom he poured out on us richly through Jesus Christ our Savior, so that being justified by his grace we might become heirs according to the hope of eternal life.

The message of grace is thoroughly Pauline as he contrasts what believers deserved because of their sin with the new life and justification that belongs to believers in Christ. Justification per se isn't mentioned in 2 Timothy 1:9, but the text is closely related since we are told that salvation isn't based on works but is ascribed to God's grace and plan from the dawn of time. We also see in Titus 2:11–14 that salvation is due to God's grace, and in 1 Timothy 1:12–16 Paul credits God's mercy and grace for saving him as the chief of sinners.

I have been making the case in this book that the biblical teaching on justification should not be limited to the word "justification." We need to cast the net wider so that we think of the concept instead of being confined by a word-study approach. Once we take this approach, it is immediately clear that 1 Corinthians 15:1–4 fits wonderfully. Paul summarizes the gospel here, and though he doesn't mention justification, the essence of justification is present. Paul declares that "Christ died for our sins" (1 Cor. 15:3) and immediately goes on to speak of his resurrection, indicating that sinners are forgiven through

Christ's death and resurrection. Nor is this a minor matter! The message proclaimed is of "first importance" (1 Cor. 15:3), and the forgiveness of sins is also associated with salvation (1 Cor. 15:2), as Paul rehearses his gospel (1 Cor. 15:1)—the message he proclaims to the world. We also see the close relationship between justification and forgiveness in Romans 4:25 (see also Col. 2:14) where Paul declares that Christ was handed over "for our trespasses and raised for our justification." Both Jesus's death and his resurrection, as in 1 Corinthians, are the basis for forgiveness of sins and for justification.

Justification reminds us that God is the one who declares us to be in the right, that forgiveness is based on his grace and mercy. Paul doesn't mention justification in 1 Thessalonians per se, but the declarations that Jesus "delivers us from the wrath to come" (1 Thess. 1:10) and that "God has not destined us for wrath, but to obtain salvation through our Lord Jesus Christ" (1 Thess. 5:9) are in the same orbit in the sense that the death of Jesus spares believers from the wrath to come. We see, then, that some who think that justification plays a minor role in Paul's thought are too tied to a word-study approach so that they miss the conceptual consistency in his thought and the prominence of the theme in the Pauline letters.

Paul doesn't talk about justification by faith in 2 Thessalonians, but it is quite fascinating to observe the many words he uses that come from the "righteous" word group (words with the Greek root *dik-*): "the righteous [*dikaias*] judgment of God" (2 Thess. 1:5); "God considers it just [*dikaion*] to repay" those who mistreat believers (1:6); "inflicting vengeance [*ekdikēsin*] on those who do not know God" (1:8); "they will suffer the punishment [*dikēn*] of eternal destruction" (1:9). Why does this matter? Because Paul refers to the final judgment, to the final assessment of the wicked, emphasizing that they will be justly condemned and sentenced, that their punishment accords with what they deserve. On the other hand, it is implied that the final judgment for believers is one in which they will not be judged and condemned but vindicated, forgiven, and acquitted. Paul doesn't specifically mention the latter, but it seems fair to say that it is implied since he thinks of the final judgment in terms of the justice of the law court.

We have been discussing the fact that some scholars have questioned the importance of justification in Paul's thinking, but when we consider the question broadly we see that justification interlocks with many key doctrines and themes, such as salvation, covenant, forgiveness, reconciliation, regeneration, eternal life, sanctification, and so on. It can't be relegated to the dustbin of Paul's thought. And we have seen a number of indications that the basic notion is present in Paul's letters even when he doesn't discuss it specifically. I will return to this matter when we consider justification and systematic theology in the last chapter.

Not by Works / Works of the Law

We come now to the texts where Paul discusses justification directly. He emphasizes that justification is by faith, and the importance of faith is clarified by the contrast with "works" or "works of the law." On eight occasions Paul declares that righteousness by "works of the law" is excluded (Rom. 3:20, 28; Gal. 2:16 [3x]; 3:2, 5, 10). What Paul means by works of the law, however, is debated.

The so-called new perspective on Paul, an understanding of Paul that began in the late 1970s (more on that later) understands works of the law to focus on boundary markers, identity badges, and ethnic distinctives such as circumcision, food laws, and Sabbath. In other words, the Jews are condemned for ethnocentrism, for requiring Gentiles to become Jews, for saying that one must accept the badges of Jewish identity to be saved. This reading of works of the law is fascinating, but interestingly enough it is not new, though with the dawn of the new perspective it appeared in new circumstances and in a new context. When the Reformers debated with Roman Catholics in the sixteenth century, the latter understood the works of the law along the same lines as those supporting the new perspective so that the works of the law were understood to be the ceremonial laws, the laws that were distinctive to Jewish believers.[5] I am not suggesting that new perspectivists are Roman Catholics; I am only noting that we find a fascinating convergence at this point.

When we examine the matter more closely, the new perspective reading of works of the law fails to convince. The term "works of the law" doesn't center on boundary markers but includes the entire law. We expect from the phrase itself that works of the law refers to the entire law, to all the works or deeds mandated by the law. It is most natural to conclude that works of the law refers to *all* the works demanded by the law. And that is what we discover when we look more closely at what Paul writes. In fact, if the emphasis lies anywhere in the phrase, Paul concentrates on the *moral failings* of the Jews.

In Romans 3:20 justification doesn't come through works of the law; instead through the law comes the knowledge of sin. What sins does Paul have in mind? Certainly, any and all sins are in his mind. It is important to recognize that Romans 3:19–20 functions as the conclusion of Romans 1:18–3:18 where the universality of sin, the comprehensive reach of sin,

5. See, e.g., John Calvin, *The Epistle of Paul the Apostle to the Romans and to the Thessalonians*, vol. 8 in *Calvin's New Testament Commentaries*, ed. D. W. Torrance and T. F. Torrance (Grand Rapids, MI: Eerdmans, 1961), 78–79; John Calvin, *The Epistles of Paul the Apostle to the Galatians, Ephesians, Philippians, and Colossians*, vol. 11 in *Calvin's New Testament Commentaries* ed. D. W. Torrance and T. F. Torrance (Grand Rapids, MI: Eerdmans, 1965), 53–55.

for both Gentiles and Jews is emphasized. When it comes to the Jews, on what basis does he indict them in this section? He doesn't say anything about excluding Gentiles. He did bring up circumcision earlier (Rom. 2:25–29), but even there he doesn't criticize them for insisting on circumcision but for disobeying the rest of the law (Rom. 2:25–27). When specific sins are mentioned, Paul includes stealing, adultery, and robbing temples (Rom. 2:21–22), and these are clearly moral norms, not boundary markers segregating Jews from Gentiles. In Romans 3:10–18 Paul cites a battery of Old Testament texts to assert that both Jews and Gentiles are under sin. Again, nothing is said about boundary markers. All are said to be unrighteous, and no person truly seeks God. He then moves to sins of speech consisting of venomous and poisonous words that strike and injure others, words of cursing and bitterness and hate. From there he moves to actions: the shedding of blood and the misery and havoc wrought in the lives of others because of sin. It is striking again that nothing is said about boundary markers or ethnic badges. A right standing before God by works is excluded in a general and broad sense, and Paul focuses on the moral evil that stains the lives of all people, both Jews and Gentiles.

The same understanding is confirmed in Galatians. Yes, the Jewish teachers in Galatians insisted that the Gentiles who had confessed Christ should be circumcised to be saved. The new perspective rightly perceives that boundary markers were an issue, that the historic religious and ethnic separation between Jews and Gentiles raised its head often in Pauline communities. So the works of the law include the boundary markers! And the new perspective reminds us that ethnic divisions concerned Paul. Peter refrained from eating with Gentiles in Antioch (Gal. 2:11–14), and thus identity badges and ethnocentrism were certainly an issue. But the new perspective wrongly puts the focus here when the reason the law doesn't save is because of the moral disobedience of all people, the failure of all to carry out the will of God. Paul's words in Galatians 2:15–21 represent both his response to Peter for ceasing to eat with the Gentiles and his words to the Galatians who are contemplating requiring circumcision for salvation. Paul reminds Peter that Jews just like Gentiles are not justified by works of the law (Gal. 2:15–16). The fundamental reason for this claim isn't because they exclude Gentiles. Paul's argument is that *as Jews*, as members of the covenant, they aren't justified by works of the law but through faith in Jesus Christ. As Jews, as members of the covenant people, they aren't justified by the law because of their sin, their disobedience.

This reading is confirmed by Galatians 3:10, a very important verse for discerning what Paul means by works of the law: "For all who rely on works of the law are under a curse; for it is written, 'Cursed be everyone who does not abide by all things written in the Book of the Law, and do them.'" We need to look at this verse carefully. Paul claims first that those who rely on works of the law are cursed. The question that we need to answer is why those who rely on works of the law are cursed. The Old Testament quotation, taken from Deuteronomy 27:26 and probably 28:58 as well, provides the reason, explaining why a curse lies on those who rely on works of the law. They are cursed because they don't do *everything* included in the law. A definition of works of the law is hidden in the text since works of the law are described in terms of *everything* (*pasin*) written in the Torah. Therefore, comprehensive obedience is required to be right with God; the curse falls on those who fail to keep all that is inscribed in the law. We find a syllogism here, though the middle term of the argument is left out:

1. One must keep the *entire law* to avoid the curse.
2. No one keeps the law *perfectly.*
3. Therefore, all those who are of works of the law are cursed.

Some have objected to this syllogism since Paul doesn't state the middle term of the argument, but there is a reason he doesn't include it.[6] Everyone who knew the Scriptures was well acquainted with the fact that no one keeps the entire law, for it is stated several places in the Old Testament (1 Kings 8:46; Prov. 20:9; Eccl. 7:20), and it is evident from the stories of the greatest heroes in the Old Testament who all failed at various points in their lives. Paul doesn't include the middle step in the argument since it was not controversial—it was often taught in the Old Testament that no one can keep the law perfectly. I conclude that works of the law refers to the entire law, and justification can't be obtained by works of the law since, as Paul says in Romans 3:23, "all have sinned and fall short of the glory of God." James concurs with this understanding, "For whoever keeps the whole law but fails in one point has become guilty of all of it" (James 2:10). Partial obedience will not do. If we ask theologically why this is so, we realize that God is morally perfect and beautiful in holiness, and thus that which is not holy and perfect cannot stand in his presence.

Paul's autobiographical reflections, as he responds to opponents in Philippians 3, also cast light on the matter. The opponents required circumcision and obedience to the law (Phil. 3:2). For Paul such mandates are a reliance on the flesh instead of the Spirit, causing one to boast in self instead of in Christ

6. Some have also said that Paul could not believe perfect obedience was required since Old Testament saints could offer sacrifices to atone for sins. Such an objection misses the salvation-historical character of Paul's argument. Now that Christ has come, Old Testament sacrifices no longer atone for sins, and thus those who rely on the law covenant must keep all its provisions to be justified, and such obedience is impossible.

Jesus (Phil. 3:3–4). He reminds the readers that he once played that very game. Indeed, he played it better than his adversaries (Phil. 3:4–6). He was circumcised on the eighth day according to the law (Lev. 12:3); he was an Israelite; he knew the tribe he was from, the tribe of Benjamin—the tribe from which the first king of Israel came; he was "a Hebrew of Hebrews"—probably meaning that he spoke Aramaic or Hebrew. Now the first part of this list has to do with ethnic matters, with boundary issues, and the new perspective isn't wrong to see such as part of the issue. After all, circumcision, food laws, and Sabbath were part of the law, and Jews doubtless looked down on Gentiles for failing to observe such. It is human nature to look down on people from other ethnic groups, and it is all the more tempting when, as the Jews thought, the other ethnic group is considered to be unclean and sinful.

But Paul doesn't restrict himself to ethnic matters in Philippians 3:4–6. He goes on to say that he is a Pharisee with respect to the law, and Paul claims elsewhere that the Pharisees are the strictest and most accurate sect with respect to the law (Acts 26:5). The argument goes beyond boundary markers in that Paul features his extraordinary devotion to observe the law—a devotion that surpassed other Jews (cf. Gal. 1:13–14). We could be confused by the next item—his persecution of the church—but the purpose is similar. Before Paul's conversion his persecution of the church revealed his devotion to Torah. In his zeal he thought he was like Phinehas who put to death the Israelite man and Midianite woman having sex near the tabernacle (Num. 25:6–8). He believed that he was zealous like Elijah who had the four hundred prophets of Baal executed (1 Kings 18:40). He was convinced that he was following the example of Mattathias who killed the Jew who was about to offer a pagan sacrifice on the altar (1 Macc. 2:19–26). Paul believed his persecution and slaying of Christians was emblematic of his devotion to God, though it was zeal without knowledge (Rom. 10:2).

Finally, Paul's obedience of the law is blameless (Phil. 3:6). This doesn't mean that his obedience was perfect since no Jews believed perfect obedience was possible for sinful people (see 1 Kings 8:46). What Paul means is that his obedience was remarkable and that he faithfully offered sacrifices for atonement when he sinned. Despite the remarkable obedience that characterized Paul's life, right standing with God didn't come from Paul's extraordinary achievements, not even his amazing devotion to the law. Paul's righteousness was deficient since it was "a righteousness of my own that comes from the law" (Phil. 3:9).

What Paul means in Philippians 3 is illuminated by Romans 9:30–10:8 since this text is parallel in many respects with Philippians 3. In Romans 10 national Israel is contemplated, while in Philippians 3 Paul's personal life is under consideration. What Paul says about himself *autobiographically* in Philippians 3 is matched by Israel *nationally* in Romans 10. According to Romans 9:31–32 many Jews pursued the law for righteousness, but they didn't attain righteousness by the law because they pursued the law from works instead of faith (Rom. 9:31–32). In their zeal they tried to establish their own righteousness instead of recognizing that righteousness comes through faith in Christ (Rom. 10:2–4). They tried to establish their righteousness by doing (Rom. 10:5) instead of by believing (Rom. 10:6–8). Paul, of course, as we shall see later, isn't opposed to good works, but works aren't sufficient to obtain righteousness in God's sight since God demands perfect obedience. So, too, Paul, according to Philippians 3, tried to establish his righteousness by his obedience to the law. When he was converted, however, he discovered that righteousness doesn't come "from the law" but "through faith in Christ"

(Phil. 3:9). Both Romans 9–10 and Philippians 3 contrast two ways of righteousness: doing versus trusting; achieving versus believing; performing versus resting.

We should notice something else about Romans 9–10, something that is crucial for the question before us. There is no reference to works of the law or to Sabbath, circumcision, or food laws. Paul refers to works (*erga*) in general, and thus we have no evidence that boundary markers or identity badges were at stake in this text. This fits with the life of Abraham as well where we are informed that he wasn't "justified by works" (Rom. 4:2). The reference isn't to works of law since Abraham didn't live under the law, and it is fascinating how many scholars fail to make this observation. When Paul says Abraham can't boast of his works in God's sight, the reason he can't brag is because he didn't do the requisite works. Abraham after all came from a family of idolaters (Josh. 24:2), and presumably he joined his family in worshiping other gods. Abraham needed justification because of his sin, and the same was true in David's case (Rom. 4:6–8). Paul cites Psalm 32 where David confesses his sins before the Lord, rejoicing in the blessedness of forgiveness (Ps. 32:1–2). David's works (Rom. 4:6) were such that he could not stand in the right before the Lord. Certainly, David's guilt didn't relate to the boundary markers; his guilt related to his sins against Bathsheba and Uriah. David's unrighteousness comes from his *moral failings*.

Paul's use of the word "works" along with the expression "works of the law" shows that his concern is fundamentally with human disobedience instead of boundary markers. Ethnocentrism is a concern—the new perspective is on to a truth here, but it isn't the fundamental criticism Paul levels against his fellow Jews. The problem with the Jews and with all people everywhere is sin, the evil and wickedness that separates human beings from God.[7] Thus, Paul affirms famously in Ephesians 2:9 that salvation isn't "a result of works," and it can't be based on works because of human disobedience.

Paul gets even more specific in Titus 3:5, remarking that God doesn't save or justify us based on "works done by us in righteousness." The additional words demonstrate that the works in question have to do with godly behavior, with actions that are pleasing to God, actions that are right and true and holy. And we know that human sin is the reason righteousness by works is excluded in Titus, for Paul says in Titus 3:3, "For we ourselves were once foolish, disobedient, led astray, slaves to various passions and pleasures, passing our days in malice and envy, hated by others and hating one another." Again, he mentions nothing about boundary markers. Sin bursts out in moral evil, in our hatred of one another. So, too, in 2 Timothy 1:9 believers are not called "because of our works" but because of God's gracious purpose in Christ Jesus. Justification can't be generated by human beings since we "were by nature children of wrath" (Eph. 2:3). All human beings are the sons and daughters of Adam (Rom. 5:12–19), and they enter the world spiritually dead and condemned before God because of their sin. One weakness in some new perspective accounts is an insufficient emphasis on the power of sin in Paul's theology.

The human condition is dire indeed. Human beings are not only sinners but are enslaved to sin (Rom. 6:6, 16, 17, 18, 20). Sin and death are the two powers that reign and rule over all human beings. Believers are under sin (Rom. 3:9; 7:14; Gal. 3:22), under the law (Rom. 6:14–15; Gal. 3:23; 4:4–5, 21; 5:18), under a curse (Gal. 3:10), under the pedagogue (Gal. 3:25), and under the elements of the world (Gal. 4:3). Sin is a

7. I am not denying, incidentally, that ethnocentricism is also a sin! The point is that it isn't the fundamental complaint lodged against the Jews.

power that reigns over all those who are in Adam. We don't come into the world vibrant and alive but "dead in . . . trespasses and sins" (Eph. 2:1 CSB; cf. Eph. 2:5). As sons and daughters of Adam, sin is the center and circumference of our lives, and thus we stand guilty before the divine judge. Human obedience, therefore, cannot qualify us to stand in a relationship with a God who is blazing in holiness, a God who is "a consuming fire" (Heb. 12:29).

Justification by Faith

Justification can't be obtained by works or works of the law since human beings are sinners. Paul emphasizes, by way of contrast, that people are justified by faith. In a verse that many consider the theme of Romans, he declares God's righteousness "is revealed from faith to faith" (Rom. 1:17 CSB), which probably means that a right relationship with God is ours by faith from first to last. Twice he quotes Habakkuk 2:4 (a verse we looked at previously), which says, "The righteous shall live by faith" (Rom. 1:17; Gal. 3:11). The centrality of faith is clear in Romans 3:22 (see also Gal. 3:22) where "the righteousness of God through faith in Jesus Christ" is "for all who believe" (cf. also Rom. 3:25–26; 5:1).

Often works are contrasted with faith, with Paul insisting that the latter is the way we receive justification (Rom. 3:27–28; Gal. 2:16, 20). Indeed, Paul contrasts believing and working in the strongest terms (Rom. 4:4–5). Those who do the works required naturally expect a reward, just as laborers expect wages for the work they have done. Paul agrees with this in principle. Those who do the necessary work deserve a reward—if the works are faithfully done, they deserve acquittal. Reward for righteousness, for obedience, isn't a problem; that is actually justice and fairness. The problem is that no one does the works mandated. All sin, and thus no one can put God in their debt. No one faithfully serves God by their labor. Thus, the only hope is for God to justify the ungodly, and he does so for those who put their faith in Christ Jesus, and Jesus's atoning death satisfies God's justice and holiness. Justification is a gift, but it is based on Christ's sacrifice where he takes the wrath of God on himself for our sake and our salvation (Rom. 3:25–26).

Paul teaches, then, that faith and works stand in fundamental opposition to one another as a way to justification (Rom. 4:13–16; Gal. 3:18). If righteousness is obtained through keeping the law, then salvation is no longer based on God's promise and faith is emptied of its significance and distinctiveness. Faith accords with God's grace since it looks to the Lord for righteousness instead of finding it in the human being. Works call attention to what human beings achieve, but faith looks to what God in Christ has done. Again, Paul doesn't have any problem with works per se. If human beings could carry out the works commanded, they would be rewarded. Adam and Eve were only punished in the garden after they sinned. God has kindly and mercifully provided another way to know him and to be related to him, and this is communicated well in Ephesians 2:8: "For by grace you have been saved through faith. And this is not your own doing; it is the gift of God." Faith is fundamentally receptive in that it looks away from self to God in Christ for righteousness, and thus Luther rightly saw that there was in this sense a passive dimension to faith. In faith we receive the righteousness of another.

The righteousness of the law stems from doing what the law mandates, but no one can fulfill what the law commands (Rom. 10:5; Gal. 3:12; Phil. 3:9). Thus, righteousness by faith looks away from ourselves to what God has done in the death and resurrection of Jesus Christ (Rom. 4:25; 10:6–8). Righteousness doesn't come by achieving but believing, not by doing but by resting in God's promises, not by performing but by trusting in Christ. In both Romans and Galatians Paul makes a point of saying that Abraham was justified by faith (Rom. 4:1–5; Gal. 3:6–9), which constitutes important evidence since Abraham was the founder, the progenitor of the Jewish people. The faith that justifies isn't limited to a particular ethnic group, as if circumcised Jews enjoy a particular advantage (Rom. 3:29–30; 4:9–12; Gal. 3:26). Even Abraham was justified by faith *before* he was circumcised (Rom. 4:9–10).

There has been a rather intense debate whether the genitive phrases *pistis Christou* and *pistis Iēsou Christou* in Paul speak of "*faith in* Christ" or the "*faithfulness of* Christ."[8] Grammatically, both are possible, and this isn't the place to enter into the discussion in detail. I suggest that the following evidence supports the traditional reading "faith in Christ." First, Jesus says in Mark 11:22, "have faith in God" (*pistin theou*). The verse doesn't make sense, despite the views of a few, if translated, "have the faithfulness of God."

Second, in some texts the verb "believing" and the phrase "faith in Christ" are both present (e.g., Rom. 3:22; Gal 3:22). The question is how we should interpret such. Some scholars think in such cases that Paul couldn't be thinking of faith in Christ since it would be superfluous to write about both "faith in Christ" *and* "believing." I suggest, on the other hand, that faith is mentioned twice because of its importance, because it is fundamental. In other words, Paul *emphasizes* faith in Christ. We should also note that the two expressions "faith in Christ" and "believing" aren't exactly synonymous. After all, in the phrase in question he stresses faith *in Christ* while the other

8. For a good entrée into the debate, see Michael F. Bird and Preston Sprinkle, eds., *The Faith of Jesus Christ: Exegetical, Biblical, and Theological Studies* (Peabody, MA: Hendrickson, 2009).

instance mentions believing in general. Faith isn't vague and elusive but is directed to Jesus Christ as one crucified on our behalf, as one who has triumphed in his resurrection over death and sin.

Third, the flow of thought in Paul's letters makes it difficult to believe that Paul refers to "faithfulness" in Galatians 3:2, 5, when the next verse (Gal. 3:6) uses the verb "believed." So too, Romans 3:21–31 is followed by Romans 4 where Paul transitions from faith in chapter 3 to Abraham's belief and trust in chapter 4. It is more natural to think that he has human faith in view in both instances.

Fourth, the contrast between works and faith in Paul points to two *human* activities. Fifth, it is also interesting to observe that Paul never uses the word "faith" to describe Jesus's obedience anywhere else in his letters, except for in 2 Timothy 2:13 where Jesus is faithful as God is faithful. Describing Jesus as faithful wasn't characteristic of Paul, but he often emphasizes human faith.

The debate over this matter will not end until the eschaton, but each interpreter must make a decision. We might even wonder why this is important, why this even matters. The answer is that our faith is in a person, in one who is fully human and fully divine, in the Messiah Jesus. The object of our faith stands out when our faith is in Jesus the Christ.

Justification Is Forensic

The historic Protestant position is that justification is forensic, that it has do with the law court, that it means that God as the judge declares sinners to be not guilty. The word "justify" doesn't mean *make righteous* but *declare righteous*. We see this forensic understanding in a number of places in the Old Testament. For instance, those who participate in lawsuits are warned, "Stay far away from a false accusation. Do not kill the innocent and the just, because I will not justify the guilty" (Ex. 23:7 CSB). The legal character of the situation is obvious, and the meaning of the word "justify" is certainly declarative. In legal cases the guilty will not be declared to be innocent. The Lord will judge according to the facts of the case and render the appropriate verdict.

We encounter a similar situation in Deuteronomy 25:1, but here the judges are human beings: "When people have a dispute, they are to take it to court and the judges will decide the case, acquitting the innocent and condemning the guilty" (NIV; see also 1 Kings 8:31–32; 2 Chron. 6:23). Judges don't *make* someone who is blameless innocent, nor do they *make* someone who has done evil wicked. Instead, they render a verdict according to the facts of the case so that they *declare* that the innocent person is righteous and the wicked person is guilty. Well, at least righteous judges adjudicate court cases fairly, but when Israel was straying from the Lord, their judges would

> acquit the guilty for a bribe,
> and deprive the innocent of his right! (Isa. 5:23)

The massive evil in such instances is captured by Proverbs 17:15:

> He who justifies the wicked and he who condemns the righteous
> are both alike an abomination to the Lord.

In context both the verb "justifies" and the verb "condemns" are declarative. The one who justifies the wicked declares the wicked to be in the right, even though they are legally liable. Similarly, the one who condemns the righteous declares that the one who has done good is guilty, even though he or she is innocent.

We have thought about Job earlier, and the forensic and declarative meaning of the term is evident in a number of texts. If we think about it, it is obvious that Job isn't asking God to *make him righteous*. Instead, Job insists that he is righteous and that the Lord should judge him according to the facts of the case.

> Behold, I have prepared my case;
> I know that I shall be in the right. (Job 13:18)

Job is convinced that he if he could argue his case before God that he would be declared to be in the right. We see the same sentiment in Job 27:6:

> I hold fast my righteousness and will not let it go;
> my heart does not reproach me for any of my days.

Elihu complains since Job insists that he is in the right and goes on to say that God is in the wrong:

> I am in the right,
> and God has taken away my right. (Job 34:5; cf. Job 40:8)

The legal character of the term also shines forth in Isaiah 43:26:

> Put me in remembrance; let us argue together;
> set forth your case, that you may be proved right.

Yahweh is eager to go to court with Israel since he is convinced that their legal case will fall apart, that it will be obvious that they are in the wrong. Jeremiah also has a complaint against the Lord and wants to file a case against him, even though he knows that the Lord will win the case!

> You will be righteous, Lord,
> even if I bring a case against you.
> Yet, I wish to contend with you. (Jer. 12:1 CSB)

The forensic meaning of the verb "justify" is also clear in Paul's letters.[9] Consider Romans 8:33: "Who shall bring any charge against God's elect? It is God who justifies." The court setting is obvious as Paul considers a legal case where a charge could be leveled hypothetically against those who belong to the Lord as his chosen ones. No accusation will stand, however, since God is the judge and the jury, and he pronounces the verdict: not guilty. Romans 2:13 is also declarative: "For it is not the hearers of the law who are righteous before God, but the doers of the law who will be justified." Paul's statement here fits with what we saw in the Old Testament. Those who do what the law commands will be declared to be in the right by the Lord.

The forensic and declarative nature of righteousness is also supported by the use of the verb "count" or "reckon" (*logizomai*) with "righteousness" in Paul (see Rom. 3:28; 4:3, 5, 9, 10, 11, 22, 23, 24; Gal. 3:6). The word "count" speaks of something being credited to one, and the accounting metaphor supports a declarative meaning. The word "count" or "credit" may be used in two different ways. Something may be credited to a person because it truly belongs to him, or conversely something may be counted or credited that isn't inherently his. We see the first instance in the case of Phinehas where we are told that his killing of an Israelite man and a Midianite woman

9. Cf. the discussion in Brendan Bryne, *Paul and the Economy of Salvation: Reading from the Perspective of the Last Judgment* (Grand Rapids, MI: Baker Academic, 2021), 35–41.

who were having sex near the tabernacle was "counted to him as righteousness" (Ps. 106:31). In this case, it was counted as righteousness because what Phinehas did was indeed righteous. On the other hand, the verb "count" can also describe a situation where something is counted as true that is not actually the case. For example, Jacob's wives were reckoned to be foreigners by Laban even though they were his daughters, members of his family (Gen. 31:15). So too in Paul: the righteousness counted to believers isn't theirs inherently and intrinsically. It is reckoned and counted to them, even though they are not righteous in themselves, in that they are sinners. We see this clearly in Romans 4 where Paul uses the word "counted" or "reckoned" (*logizomai*), declaring that those who have transgressed, those who have failed to do the requisite works, are blessed with righteousness (Rom. 4:6, 8). They are reckoned to be righteous because of their union with Christ, which is theirs by faith.

Justification doesn't and can't come by works of the law since all are sinners (Rom. 3:20), and thus justification is by faith (Rom. 3:28; 5:1). Paul teaches something quite extraordinary, something almost unimaginable: those who are guilty—if they put their faith in Jesus Christ—will be declared to be righteous; they will be acquitted and cleared of all wrong. In teaching this, Paul seems to run afoul of Proverbs 17:15 where it is detestable to declare that the guilty are righteous, but God doesn't violate justice in declaring sinners to be in the right. Paul teaches in a number of texts that Jesus died in the place of sinners, taking on himself the wrath sinners deserved (e.g., Rom. 3:24–26; 2 Cor. 5:21; Gal. 3:13), and thus God doesn't violate justice. In the cross of Jesus Christ, God's holiness and love are both displayed.

Some scholars have argued that the verb "justify" (*dikaioō*) is forensic, while the noun "righteousness" (*dikaiosynē*), especially when it has to do with the righteousness of God, has a transformative sense. We have already seen, however, that the noun "righteousness" when it is used with the verb "reckon / count" should be understood forensically. In chapter 6 I will respond to those who understand God's righteousness as transformative and defend the notion that the noun is forensic in these cases as well.

Imputed Righteousness

A question that is often raised is whether Paul taught imputed righteousness. Some famous pastors and scholars have doubted whether imputed righteousness accords with Pauline teaching, including Richard Baxter, Robert Gundry, and N. T. Wright.[10] Despite the doubts and objections of some, there are good reasons for thinking that imputed righteousness is authentically Pauline. For instance, in Romans 5:12–19 Paul contrasts Adam and Christ. Adam and Christ function as the two covenant heads for all of humanity. Adam as the federal head brought sin, death, and condemnation to all people. Christ, on the other hand, brought life and justification to all those who are united with him by faith. Adam's one sin led to "condemnation for everyone" (CSB), while Christ's "one righteous act" accomplished "justification" (Rom. 5:18). The one righteous act here probably denotes Christ's obedience and sacrifice accomplished at the cross. Still, this one act of righteousness can't be segregated ultimately from Christ's life of obedience. His one act of obedience at the cross wouldn't have any effect if his life previous to

10. On Baxter, see Hans Boersma, *A Hot Pepper Corn: Richard Baxter's Doctrine of Justification in Its Seventeenth-Century Context of Controversy* (Zoetermeer: Uitgeverij Boekencentrum, 1993), esp. 257–330; Tim Cooper, *John Owen, Richard Baxter and the Formation of Nonconformity* (Burleigh, VT: Ashgate, 2011), esp. 75–80. For Gundry, see Robert H. Gundry, "The Nonimputation of Christ's Righteousness," in *Justification: What's at Stake in the Current Debates*, ed. M. A. Husbands and D. J. Trier (Downers Grove, IL: IVP Academic, 2004), 17–45. Wright's view on imputation will be explored in chapter 6.

the cross were stained through sin. His obedience on the cross climaxed a life characterized by complete devotion and submission to the will of God. When we trust in Christ for salvation, the entirety of who Christ is, the whole Christ, is given to believers. Luther often said that believers are married to Christ, and when we are united to him then all of Christ, all that he is, is given to believers, and that includes his righteousness.[11]

We see imputation as well in Romans 5:19: "For as by the one man's disobedience the many were made sinners, so by the one man's obedience the many will be made righteous." The verbs translated "made" here derive from the Greek word *kathistēmi*, which often has the meaning "appoint" (Matt. 24:45, 47; 25:21, 23; Luke 12:14, 42, 44; Acts 6:3; 7:10, 27; Titus 1:5; Heb. 5:1; 7:28; 8:3), and there are good reasons for assigning the same meaning here. Such an understanding fits with federal headship where Adam and Christ are appointed as the covenant heads for human beings. Since Adam is our covenant head, we are constituted as sinners because we are united with him. Similarly, those who have received "the free gift of righteousness" (Rom. 5:17) are constituted as righteous because they are united to Christ who serves as their covenant head. To put it another way, the righteousness of believers is perfect because their righteousness isn't in themselves but in Christ crucified and risen.

I noted above that in Romans 4 Paul often emphasizes that our faith is counted (*logizomai*) as righteousness, and thus the terminology used supports imputed righteousness. It is imperative to see the flow of thought in Romans 3–4. What Paul says about being righteous by faith follows the crucial and central paragraph in Romans 3:21–26 where the forgiveness of

11. See Martin Luther, "Two Kinds of Righteousness," in *Martin Luther: Selections from His Writings*, ed. John Dillenberger (Garden City, NY: Doubleday, 1961), 87.

believers is grounded in the atoning death of Christ, where God (because of his great love) sent his Son (who gladly came because of his love) to take on himself the punishment of our sins. Thus, believers are justified before God and redeemed from their sins because of God's gracious and merciful love, for in the cross God's holiness is revealed and his love is manifested. How does this relate to imputation?

When Paul says that we are righteous by faith, we should not understand him to say that faith *is* our righteousness, as if faith is a virtue by which we are counted as righteous. The text could be construed to say that faith *is* our righteousness, but in context faith should be understood as an instrument, as a vehicle by which Christ becomes our righteousness. Faith is like the electric cord that transmits electricity to a lamp or a computer or any other device that uses electricity. The cord transmits the electricity, connecting the device to a source of power. Since our righteousness is a gift of God (Rom. 5:17; 10:3; Phil. 3:9), faith is the means, the cord, by which Christ's righteousness is granted to us. Such an understanding of righteousness makes sense theologically since at the end of the day it isn't our faith that saves us but God himself. This is another way of saying that ultimately our faith doesn't save us; it is the object of faith that saves us. If we think of it this way, imputation makes sense because we all recognize that if we put our faith in the wrong object, our faith is useless and futile. Thus, our faith saves because it unites us to Christ.

I return to a verse I mentioned previously, but here we need to consider its implications for imputation. The verse is 2 Corinthians 5:21: "For our sake he made him to be sin who knew no sin, so that in him we might become the righteousness of God." The great exchange here points to our imputation. Paul, however, doesn't refer to the righteousness of Christ but to the righteousness of God. This observation is obviously correct, but we should not miss the fact that the righteousness of God becomes ours "in him"—that is, in Christ. God's righteousness is granted to us through the cross of Christ, through the one who became sin for us. Christ took our sin upon himself in the cross so that, as we are united to Christ, we receive the righteousness of God. This is the great exchange that was explained so beautifully, as we saw earlier, in the Epistle of Diognetus (9:2–5).

Conclusion

In this chapter we have considered Paul's teaching on justification, and we have seen that the doctrine plays a crucial role in Paul's theology. Justification can't be achieved through works, through human obedience—not even the works commanded by the law—because all without exception are sinners. Justification, being right with God, is, as is evident in the case of Abraham, by faith, and this faith is particularly in Jesus Christ. Justification is to be defined forensically, as the meaning of the verb stems from the law court where the one in the right is acquitted, declared to be righteous. The righteousness that belongs to believers is imputed, credited to the account of those who put their trust in Christ. They are righteous because, in being united to Jesus Christ, all that is his is now theirs. Christ took the punishment we deserve, and in turn we receive his righteousness and stand holy and blameless before him.

5

Justification in the Rest of the New Testament

In this chapter we will consider justification by faith in the remainder of the New Testament, which includes Acts, the General Epistles, and Revelation. It is well-known that we don't find the same focus on justification that is present in Paul, but this book advances the theme that justification should not be restricted to a word-study approach, that the concept is present even when the word is absent. When we take a broader perspective, we see that the notion of justification is present more than one might expect. Given the scattered nature of the references, I will proceed corpus by corpus and reserve discussion of the epistle of James for last.

Acts of the Apostles

Justification is scarcely front and center in Acts, but it is often emphasized that salvation comes by faith (Acts 3:16; 4:4, 32; 8:12, 13; 9:42; 10:43; 11:17, 21; 13:12, 39, 41, 48; 14:1, 9, 23, 27; 15:7, 9, 11; 16:31, 34; 17:12, 34; 18:8, 27; 19:2, 4,

9, 18; 20:21; 21:20, 25; 22:19; 24:24; 26:18; 28:24). At the same time those hearing the message were summoned to turn to the Lord and to repent (Acts 2:38; 3:19; 8:22; 14:15; 15:19; 17:30; 26:18, 20; 28:27). Believing and repenting are two sides of the same coin, and thus we should not privilege belief over against repentance. Still, the emphasis in Acts clearly lies on believing, for words associated with repentance occur around twenty times, but words associated with believing more than fifty times. The focus on believing is even more evident when we recognize that Christians in Acts are identified as "believers" (or "those who believed") on quite a few occasions (Acts 2:44; 4:4, 32; 5:14; 10:45; 15:5; 19:18; 21:20; 22:19), signifying that belief particularly characterizes Christians. The prominence of faith and believing accords with Paul's claim that righteousness is by faith alone.

A few texts will be considered briefly. We see in Acts 8:12 that the Samaritans believed as Philip "preached good news about the kingdom of God and the name of Jesus Christ." Their trust and faith, then, were particularly in Jesus Christ. Another striking text is Acts 10:43 where Peter was preaching to Cornelius and his friends. As Peter concluded his sermon, he declared, "Everyone who believes in him receives forgiveness of sins." The object of faith is Jesus Christ, but it is also illuminating that those who believe are forgiven of their sins. The term "justification" isn't used here, but Paul forged a close link between justification and forgiveness in Romans 4:2–8 (cf. also Col. 2:14) since forgiveness means that the sins committed are no longer held against one, that sins are remitted and forgotten. To say that one who believes receives forgiveness, then, is close to saying that justification is by faith. Indeed, Peter doesn't exhort Cornelius and his Gentile friends to observe the Torah or to pursue moral virtue to be right with God but to receive forgiveness of sins. In fact, as the entire account reveals (Acts 10:1–11:18) the Jews were quite astonished that the Gentiles received the Spirit without adhering to the Torah.

Another central text is Acts 15:7–11. Here the church convened a council at Jerusalem to determine whether Gentiles were required to keep the law and receive circumcision to be saved (Acts 15:1, 5). The Old Testament was quite clear that one must be circumcised to belong to the covenant people (Gen. 17:9–14; Ex. 4:24–26; Lev. 12:3). The issue, then, was whether one was required to observe the Torah, the Old Testament law, to be a member of the people of God. In Acts 15:7–11 Peter arose and recalled his visit to Cornelius and his friends, which may have been ten years earlier, remembering that God had granted the Gentiles the Spirit in the same way as he had bestowed the Spirit on the Jews. Peter declared that the Lord "cleansed their hearts by faith" (Acts 15:9). In fact, mandating observance of the law would place a "yoke" on the Gentiles that the Jews, both past and present, weren't able to keep (Acts 15:10). Peter agrees with Paul that salvation doesn't come via the law since human beings were unable to keep the law. Instead of keeping the law for salvation, people receive new life "through the grace of the Lord Jesus" (Acts 15:11). We see something that is very much like Paul's understanding of justification here. Salvation doesn't come through keeping the law because human beings are sinners. Instead, Peter puts "faith" and "grace" together as the way of salvation. Salvation by faith accords with God's grace since faith and trust look away from self to God himself, to God's power and mercy rather than to the ability of the human being. This formulation comes rather close to Ephesians 2:8 where Paul affirms that salvation is by grace through faith. We must also recall the context since Peter clearly teaches that circumcision and the law are not required for salvation. Instead, salvation comes by grace as human beings put their trust in Jesus.

The final text I want to examine in Acts is found near the end of Paul's synagogue sermon in Pisidian Antioch (Acts 13:38–39). This is the only occasion where Luke reproduces an outline of the sermon Paul preached in the synagogue, and he probably included it because it represented what Paul typically preached in the synagogues. We should also note that Peter's sermon on Pentecost in Acts 2 and Paul's synagogue sermon in Acts 13 are remarkably similar in content. Luke may have included both to demonstrate that Peter and Paul preached the same gospel.

Still, with all the commonalities between the two speeches, a distinctive element emerges in Acts 13:38–39: "Let it be known to you therefore, brothers, that through this man forgiveness of sins is proclaimed to you, and by him everyone who believes is freed from everything from which you could not be freed by the law of Moses." The ESV cited above translates the two uses of the verb *dikaioō* as "freed," but the CSB has a better rendering: "Therefore, let it be known to you, brothers and sisters, that through this man forgiveness of sins is being proclaimed to you. Everyone who believes is justified through him from everything that you could not be justified from through the law of Moses." Here we have a genuine Pauline touch since he speaks of *justification*. We also see that forgiveness of sins and justification are closely associated, suggesting again that forgiveness is another way of describing justification. Furthermore, forgiveness and justification come from believing and trusting, and not through the law of Moses. Paul explicitly rejects the notion that forgiveness and justification can be obtained through the Torah. Instead, the Torah led to judgment since the law revealed the sins of human beings, showing that no one could keep its prescriptions. We have, then, a remarkable statement on justification by faith instead of by the law. We see, then, that Acts, though it doesn't center on the term "justification," sounds very much like Paul at some significant points in the narrative. Salvation comes by grace through faith and not by the law. Those who believe are saved, not those who attempt to keep the Torah.

The Epistle to the Hebrews

The epistle to the Hebrews never mentions justification, at least in its verbal form, explicitly. Still, the content of the letter fits well within the orbit of Paul's theology of justification. The realm of discourse differs, but the author maintains that the Levitical priesthood and the law didn't bring perfection (Heb. 7:11–12, 18–19). By this the author means that the law and priesthood didn't grant access to God. Jesus's one sacrifice, in contrast to the sacrifices offered under the old covenant, was effective (Heb. 9:11–28) and secured forgiveness. Old covenant priests stood and repeatedly offered the same sacrifices, but Jesus sat down at the right hand of God after offering one sacrifice (Heb. 10:1–18) so that believers may boldly enter God's presence. One of the author's favorite words is "better." With Jesus there is a "better hope" (Heb. 7:19), a "better covenant" (Heb. 7:22; cf. 8:6), and a "better" sacrifice (Heb. 9:23) so that believers look forward to "a better possession" (Heb. 10:34) and "a better country" (Heb. 11:16). The old covenant has passed away and a new covenant has arrived (Heb. 8:7–13; 10:15–18). This new covenant brings forgiveness of sins, something that was never accomplished fully and definitively under the old covenant.

The author of Hebrews, then, doesn't major on the word "justification," but his view of the covenants and the claim that forgiveness of sins comes through the death of Christ matches Pauline themes. Indeed, even though Paul probably did not write Hebrews, we can see theologically why some in the history of interpretation placed Hebrews in the Pauline corpus. Perhaps we can stretch out a bit further and notice that the writer of Hebrews typically uses the term "sanctification" in terms of *definitive* sanctification instead of *progressive* sanctification. In other words, believers are in the realm of the holy; they are holy positionally before God. Thus, the author can say, that believers "have been sanctified through the offering of the body of Jesus Christ once for all" (Heb. 10:10).[1] They are in the realm of the holy not because of their own godliness and virtue but because of the sacrifice of Christ. Similarly, he claims that the blood of Christ, his death, has sanctified believers (Heb. 10:29; 13:12). When we recall that the language of the cult and the temple predominates in Hebrews, preference for the metaphor of sanctification instead of justification is understandable. Still, the idea is substantially the same that we find in Paul's theology of justification: holiness belongs to believers through the work of Christ, and in Christ it is perfect and complete.

Another fascinating convergence between Paul and the author of Hebrews crops up when we consider the centrality of faith in Hebrews. The connection is even more suggestive since the author of Hebrews, like Paul (Rom. 1:17; Gal. 3:11), also quotes Habakkuk 2:4: "My righteous one shall live by faith" (Heb. 10:38). Here we find a specific link between being righteous and believing, and it seems that the meaning, especially when we recall that the cross achieves salvation, is quite similar to Paul's. Righteousness belongs to those who trust in the Lord, to those who depend on him.

1. The ESV reads the participle *tous hagiazomenous* in Heb. 10:14 as progressive ("those who are being sanctified"), but the CSB interpretation ("those who are sanctified") is preferable here. In both instances (10:10 and 10:14) the author has in mind definitive sanctification.

The reference to being righteous by faith is also placed at a critical juncture in the letter since the author moves on in Hebrews 11 to his famous chapter on faith. We can immediately say that faith can't be dismissed as a minor theme in the letter. Indeed, we are told that those who exercise faith are commended by God (Heb. 11:2, 4, 39). The word for "commended" (*martyreō*) isn't synonymous with "justified," but it comes from the world of the law court where there is testimony and witness bearing so that the approval spoken of has a legal flavor. We can go another step because in the case of Abel we are told that he was commended as "righteous" (*dikaios*, Heb. 11:4). One might say that Abel was righteous because of the gifts he offered, but the author emphasizes the priority of his faith, indicating that faith was foundational and the root of any good done by Abel. The author doesn't feature Abel's virtue but his faith. We are also told that Noah in building the ark "became an heir of the righteousness that comes by faith" (Heb. 11:7). It would certainly be a mistake to cut the cord between faith and obedience, as if the latter didn't matter. Still, the author focuses on faith as the guiding motive of Noah's life, as the wellspring from which obedience stemmed. He doesn't contrast faith and works as Paul does, but we should recognize that he addresses a unique situation, that his addressees faced circumstances that differed from those confronted in Romans, Galatians, and Philippians. We will see in due course that Paul also prized good works, agreeing that they flowed from faith. What we see in Hebrews is that a right relation with God finds its roots in faith, and in that respect the letter is quite similar to Paul.

The centrality of faith stands out since the author contends that no one can please God without faith (Heb. 11:6). There is another interesting connection that should be noted. When we read the Old Testament accounts of many of those mentioned in Hebrews 11, the narrative in the Old Testament context emphasizes their obedience, whether we are talking about Abel, Enoch, Noah, Abraham, Sarah, or others. The author of Hebrews, however, provides a fascinating window into the roots of the obedience of all these luminaries. In every instance, we are told that their concrete act of obedience came from their faith (Heb. 11:4, 5, 7, 8, 9, 11, 17, 20, 21, 22, 23, 24, 27, 28, 29, 30, 31, 33). Perhaps we should lift out one of these in particular: Abraham "by faith obeyed" in leaving his homeland and traveling to the land of promise (Heb. 11:8). Genesis 12 says nothing about Abraham's faith, and it rightly stresses his act of obedience in doing what the Lord commanded. Still, the author of Hebrews considers the root from which the obedience came, the motivation that sustained the sacrificial act (cf. Heb. 11:17). Obedience, as Hebrews 11 attests repeatedly, flows from faith, from trust in God, from reliance on his promises and presence. Again, the connection with Paul is patent. There is no true faith without obedience, but obedience that pleases God flows from a belief that God "rewards those who seek him" (Heb. 11:6).

1–2 Peter and Jude

Justification isn't a prime topic in these letters. Still, the grace of God is featured in a way that accords with the notion that salvation is God's work. Thus, believers are foreknown and elected by God, and the definitive sanctification by which believers are placed into the realm of the holy comes from the work of the Spirit (1 Pet. 1:1–2; 2:9). Along the same lines, believers are born again because of God's mercy and are entitled to an inheritance that can't be despoiled (1 Pet. 1:3–5; 2:10). Forgiveness of sins—that is, spiritual healing for the soul—is traced to the death of Christ on a tree (cf. Deut. 21:23) where he bore the sins of his people (1 Pet. 2:23–24). Peter draws on Isaiah 53 where the servant of the Lord carries the spiritual wounds and sicknesses of his people (Isa. 53:4, 12). Another text that stands out is 1 Peter 3:18, and here righteousness language is used: "Christ also suffered once for sins, the righteous for the unrighteous, that he might bring us to God." We clearly have the notion of substitution here, of Christ as the righteous and Holy One dying in place of the unrighteous, taking their sins upon himself. The text teaches that believers become righteous because of the cross-bearing work of Jesus, because their sins are forgiven.

Second Peter is brief, and yet we find at the outset of the letter that believers "through the righteousness of our God and Savior Jesus Christ" are recipients of "a faith equal to ours" (2 Pet. 1:1 CSB). Righteousness, as in Paul, refers to the saving righteousness of God, to the deliverance and salvation accomplished by Jesus Christ, who is identified as God and Savior in this verse. Peter, like Paul, stresses that this righteousness is ours through faith.

Jude, on the other hand, doesn't refer to justification, and this is hardly surprising given the brevity and circumstantial nature of the letter. Still, we find that the letter is bounded and framed by God's work in Christ. Thus, believers are called, loved, and kept by God the Father and Jesus Christ (Jude 1). The letter concludes with the promise that God who is the Savior through Jesus the Christ will preserve his own to the last day so that they will stand joyfully and blamelessly before God on the day of judgment (Jude 24–25). Even though justification isn't mentioned, the standing believers enjoy in God's presence depends on God's grace, on his keeping power, on his saving work. If we think of 1–2 Peter and Jude as a whole, we can rightly say that salvation is of the Lord, that it can be traced to his work so that it can't be ascribed to the goodness of human beings, and in that sense it is compatible with Pauline teaching.

The Johannine Letters

The letters of John don't feature justification either, and yet John's message in 1 John fits remarkably well with what we find in Paul's letters. Believers enjoy fellowship with God and Jesus Christ and with one another because "the blood of Jesus his Son cleanses us from all sin" (1 John 1:7). We don't find the term "justification," but the conception is remarkably similar in 1 John 1:9–2:2. Believers don't earn or merit their salvation by their virtue. Instead, when we "confess our sins, he is faithful and righteous to forgive us our sins and to cleanse us from all unrighteousness" (1 John 1:9 CSB). The image of forgiveness, as we noted previously in discussing Paul's view, is another way of talking about justification. Indeed, believers are purified of "all unrighteousness" (*pasēs adikias)*. How is this purification, cleansing, and forgiveness achieved? John answers that query in 1 John 2:1–2: Jesus as "the righteous one" (*dikaion*, CSB) functions as our advocate, and he is the appeasement (*hilasmos*), the propitiatory sacrifice for the sins we committed. The parallel with Paul is quite striking since we have the notion here that the righteous one died as a propitiatory sacrifice for the ungodly to secure forgiveness of sins (cf. Rom. 3:24–26).

Similarly, the sending of the Son by God was designed to give life to those who were in the realm of death (1 John 4:9). Once again, this death is traced to our sins (1 John 4:10), to the disobedience and lawlessness that characterizes human existence (1 John 3:4). Jesus came to remove sins (1 John 3:5) and "to destroy the works of the devil" (1 John 3:8), and John restates the notion that our sins are removed through the propitiatory and appeasing work of Jesus (1 John 4:10). Salvation doesn't come from us since "the Father has sent his Son to be the Savior of the world" (1 John 4:14). Believers may be calm, confident, full of assurance, and free from fear (1 John 4:17), resting in the assurance that "perfect love drives out fear" so that we will escape punishment on the last day (1 John 4:18 CSB). Our boldness doesn't come from anything we have done or accomplished, but "we love because he first loved us" (1 John 4:19). All of this fits with the purpose of the letter: John writes so that his readers will be assured that they have eternal life (1 John 5:13) since they belong to the Son (1 John 5:12). Such confidence and joy on the day of judgment accords with what Paul teaches about justification, though John expresses these notions in his own distinctive way.

The Book of Revelation

The book of Revelation doesn't really discuss justification in any significant sense but emphasizes the need for perseverance in order to obtain a final reward. And yet at key points in the narrative the centrality of the cross for salvation leaps out to us as readers. For instance, we see in the initial grace and peace wish (Rev. 1:4–6) that though sins bedevil and enslave human beings, believers have been set free or liberated "by his blood" (Rev. 1:5). We don't have the legal language of justification, but what is clear is that freedom from sin's bondage has been achieved through Christ's death. John strategically places this truth at the inception of the book, showing how fundamental and important it is for the lives of believers.

The unfolding of the narrative in Revelation, the structure of the book, plays a decisive role in interpreting its message. Thus, we have the programmatic vision of Christ in Revelation 1 and then the messages to the churches in Revelation 2–3, followed by the throne room vision in Revelation 4–5. Revelation 4 opens with John being transported to heaven where there is a massive thunderstorm in the throne room with strange and heavenly creatures guarding God's presence and overseeing all of creation. John sees the Lord on his throne, glorious and ineffable, ruling as the sovereign creator and monarch over the entire universe. God is seated on his throne in Revelation 5 with a seven-sealed scroll in his hand, and John weeps since no one is able to open the scroll and to disclose its contents. The opening of the scroll is crucial because it contains God's plan for history and for human beings. No one in all of creation can open the scroll except for "the Lion of the tribe of Judah, the Root of David" (Rev. 5:5). As the Davidic Messiah, as the one who fulfills God's covenant promise, he is able to open the scroll. John is *told* about the Lion and descendant of David, but when he looks he *sees* a slaughtered Lamb that is now standing (Rev. 5:6). The image of the Lamb pictures for us that the victory has been won not through lion-like strength but lamb-like sacrifice, not through destroying one's enemies but suffering and dying for them. The slaying of the Lamb represents the key to history since "by [his] blood [he] ransomed people for God from every tribe and language and people and nation" (Rev. 5:9). We see again in the narrative that the triumph of human beings—the means by which they can function as priests and kings (Rev. 5:10; cf. 1:6)—is the death of Christ.

In Revelation 7:9–17 John sees an uncountable multitude who have white robes and palm branches. As the vision concludes, they are in God's temple, inhabiting the new creation, a place where there is no hunger, thirst, or heat. Every tear is removed from their eyes, as they have come out of "the great tribulation" (Rev. 7:14). But what accounts for the great reward and blessing bestowed on this innumerable crowd? How do we explain their inclusion in the new creation? The fundamental answer is found in Revelation 7:14: "They have washed their robes and made them white in the blood of the Lamb." John doesn't use the term "justification," but he does emphasize that those who enter the new creation do so because their sins are cleansed by Christ's blood, and thus their goodness isn't the basis of their inclusion.

We find a similar theme in Revelation 12, which is a most fascinating account. Two amazing signs appeared in the heavens, first a glorious woman and then a frightening dragon. As the story continues it is evident that the woman represents the people of God and that the dragon stands for Satan. The dragon's aim is to destroy and devastate God's people. Suddenly a war in heaven breaks out where the dragon and his angels enter into combat with Michael and his angels. As a result of the battle, the dragon is cast out of heaven and flung to the earth along with his supporting angels. But why was the dragon evicted from heaven? Revelation 12:11 provides the key. The saints "have conquered" the dragon "by the blood of the Lamb" and by their testimony and willingness to lay down their lives for Christ's sake. The focus here is on the first truth: believers overcome and triumph because of Christ's blood. If we read the narrative of Revelation 12 carefully, the dragon was removed from heaven because the child of the woman (i.e., the Christ!) conquered Satan through his death and resurrection, and thus he was exalted as ruler of the world (Rev. 12:5). Satan was kicked out of the heavenlies, and thus he no longer had any standing to accuse believers before God though previously he "accuse[d] them day and night before our God" (Rev. 12:10).

The relevance for our theme should be apparent. John doesn't use the language of justification, but the text bristles with legal themes since the dragon was accusing the saints in the heavenlies, contending that they were guilty and unworthy to enter God's presence. But the charges and condemnation have no standing any longer since the Lamb shed his blood for the sake of the saints. The devil has been summarily dismissed from the heavenly courts because his condemnation no longer has any basis. John's narrative is another way of expressing the Pauline assertion, "There is therefore now no condemnation for those who are in Christ Jesus" (Rom. 8:1). This is not to say that John articulates justification the way Paul does. He presents his theology within his visionary world and in his own idiom, including distinctive themes and emphases. Still, the notion that believers are saved through the forgiveness of their sins, through the redeeming work of Christ so that they are no longer condemned before God, reminds us of what Paul teaches.

James and Justification by Works

The discussion on justification has been intense since the time of the Reformation, and understandably James's words on justification have attracted interest because he seems to differ so remarkably from Paul's perspective. Martin Luther famously expressed severe doubts about the epistle of James,[2] but he didn't argue for removing it from the canon, and his understanding of the letter is often misunderstood. Whatever we make of Luther, we still have to explicate how James's writing integrates with Paul's teaching on justification. Before we launch into considering James, we should remind ourselves of what he actually writes.

James asserts that faith without works can't save anyone (James 2:14). Without works faith is "dead" (James 2:17, 26) and "useless" (James 2:20), just as it is meaningless to wish good fortune to people without food and clothing while one does

2. Martin Luther, *Word and Sacrament I*, ed. E. Theodore Bachmann, vol. 35 of *Luther's Works* (Philadelphia: Muhlenberg, 1960), 395–97.

nothing to supply their needs (James 2:15–16). James contends that both Abraham (James 2:21) and Rahab (James 2:25) were justified by their works—Abraham by offering Isaac, Rahab by welcoming and protecting the Israelite spies. Thus, faith is brought to its completion and realization by works (James 2:22). Furthermore, Abraham being counted as righteous is fulfilled by the works that he did.

Historical-critical scholars often claim that James and Paul contradict one another.[3] They assert that we need to read texts objectively, and it is quite clear that James and Paul diametrically oppose one another. The arguments in favor of this view are quite straightforward in that Paul teaches justification by faith apart from works, and James says that faith without works doesn't justify. Furthermore, Paul cites Genesis 15:6 to say that Abraham was justified by faith instead of works (Rom. 4:3; Gal. 3:6), while James quotes the same verse in support of justification by works. Furthermore, Romans 3:28 teaches that we are justified by faith alone, but James specifically says "a person is justified by works and not by faith alone" (James 2:24). We can certainly understand why some scholars think James and Paul contradict one another, but there are good grounds for rejecting this view.

Let me begin by noting that both the epistle of James and the Pauline letters were recognized to be inspired and canonical in the early church, and thus early Christians didn't see any contradiction between the two. The historic Christian view is that the Scriptures are the inspired word of God and thus are completely true in everything they teach. Scholarship since the Enlightenment has privileged human reason, particularly

3. E.g., Martin Hengel ("Der Jakobusbrief als antipaulinische Polemik," in *Tradition and Interpretation in the New Testament: Essays in Honor of E. Earle Ellis for His 60th Birthday*, ed. Gerald F. Hawthorne with Otto Betz [Grand Rapids, MI: Eerdmans, 1987], 248–65) argues that James and Paul hold contradictory views on justification.

emphasizing contradictions in scriptural texts. Such readings stand in conflict with Christian orthodoxy and represent a different philosophical stance from that which is taken by those who subscribe to the authority and the truthfulness of the Scriptures. This is not to say that those who are orthodox don't give reasons or evidence in support of their views. I will present below three different ways of solving the apparent contradiction, and I will defend a variant of the third view.

A few have maintained that when James speaks of being saved (James 2:14) and justified by works (James 2:21, 24, 25) that salvation and justification here are not soteric realities at all.[4] In other words, the terms "save" and "justify" have very different meanings from what they have in Paul where a right relationship with God is intended, where eternal life is at stake. Instead, on this reading James speaks of enjoying a fruitful life as a disciple of Christ. A life of obedience brings joy and fulfillment as one lives on earth, but it is unnecessary for participating in life in the age to come. Virtually all interpreters agree that this interpretation is deeply flawed and quite improbable. We have no evidence that the verbs "save" and "justify" should be relegated to a fruitful life on earth. Indeed, it is difficult to believe that such words have a meaning that differs so dramatically from their usage in Paul and in the remainder of the New Testament. We can safely dismiss this interpretation as special pleading.

The next reading is much more plausible, representing the historic Roman Catholic reading of the text, or at least the reading that has been supported since the Reformation. Interpreters attempt to explain how Paul and James cohere when Paul says believers aren't justified by works, while James contends works

4. See e.g., Earl D. Radmacher, "First Response to 'Faith according to the Apostle James' by John F. MacArthur Jr," *Journal of the Evangelical Theological Society* 33 (1990): 35–41.

are necessary for justification. Roman Catholics have solved the puzzle by claiming that James and Paul mean different things by the term "works." On first glance the Roman Catholic view seems to be correct since James clearly says justification isn't by faith alone. When Paul affirms that we aren't justified by works, he means, according to the traditional Roman Catholic reading, that we aren't justified by the works of the law, and the phrase "works of the law" refers to the *ceremonial law*, to the law that segregated Jews from Gentiles. James, on the other hand, has the *moral law* in his sights when he claims that we are justified by works. It is quite easy to see, in this Roman Catholic reading, that there isn't a genuine contradiction between the two writers. According to this interpretation, justification is based on our moral works, on the goodness and virtue of human beings. Paul merely insists that human beings don't have to keep the ceremonial law to be justified, and thus things like food and purity laws and circumcision aren't mandated for salvation.

The typical Roman Catholic solution certainly works logically and makes sense, although readers should know that not all Roman Catholic scholars today agree with this reading.[5] The contemporary Roman Catholic Church has many members in it who don't necessarily endorse the official doctrinal statements of the church, but that is a story for another place and another time. Even though the traditional Roman Catholic interpretation is sensible and clear, I would argue that it fails exegetically. In other words, its interpretation of the text is not persuasive. I am not going to rehearse the discussion of "works of the law" found in chapter 5, but there we saw that

5. See, e.g., Ulrich Wilckens, *Der Brief an die Römer*, Teilband 1: *Röm 1–5*, Evangelisch-Katholischer Kommentar zum Neuen Testament 6/1 (Zurich: Benziger, 1978), 120–21; J. A. Fitzmyer, "Paul's Jewish Background and the Deeds of the Law," in *According to Paul: Studies in the Theology of the Apostle* (New York: Paulist, 1993), 23.

works of the law can't be restricted to the ceremonial law. The works of the law in Paul refer to the entire law, and thus the Catholic assertion that Paul limits himself to the ceremonial law isn't convincing. Even if one were to believe that works of the law refers only to the ceremonial law, there is a further problem with the Roman Catholic reading since Paul often says that justification and salvation don't come by "works" (Rom. 4:2, 4, 6; 9:11, 32; 11:6; Eph. 2:9; 2 Tim. 1:9; Titus 3:5) and there is no reference to the law in these texts. In these verses the term "works" is general and naturally includes anything and everything a person might do to achieve life eternal. Thus, there is no basis for limiting what Paul says about justification to the ceremonial law, showing that the Roman Catholic reading fails because it doesn't explain convincingly Paul's claim that justification can't be obtained by works.

Often Reformed interpreters posit a distinction in the word "justify" (*dikaioō*) in discriminating between the intentions of Paul and James. Thus, they affirm that in Paul the term means "declare righteous," while in James it means "show to be righteous" or "prove to be righteous."[6] On these terms, Paul says that believers are declared to be righteous before God apart from works, while James doesn't have in mind a legal declaration. According to this reading "justify" in James means that one is shown, demonstrated, or proved to be righteous by works so that works function as the evidence or corroboration of one's justification. Theologically, I agree with this reading, but lexically it is less persuasive. We don't have clear evidence that the verb "justify" means "demonstrate" or "prove" in James, and we saw earlier that the legal meaning of the term "justify" predominates. Actually, a legal understanding of the

6. E.g., R. C. Sproul, *Faith Alone: The Evangelical Doctrine of Justification* (Grand Rapids, MI: Baker, 1995), 166.

term makes good sense in James since works vindicate one before God—works acquit one in the divine law court. We don't have any clear indication from the way the verb "justify" is typically used in the Scriptures or from the context in James that it should be given a distinct meaning from what it has in Paul, and thus the solution should be rejected as exegetically and lexically unpersuasive.

I suggest another option. The difference isn't in the meaning of the terms "works" or "justify" since these words most likely have the same meaning in both Paul and James.[7] The difference lies in what the two authors mean by *faith*. Before I elaborate on this, other important features that bear on the interpretation of the matter before us should be considered. For instance, when interpreting letters, it is necessary to recognize the different circumstances and situations that are addressed in the letters in question. Epistles typically respond to particular circumstances, so discerning the situation that calls forth a letter is imperative since what an author writes is directed to the church or churches addressed. Thus, when Paul says that we are not justified by works, he responds to legalism—the notion that one can stand in the right before God on the basis of works. By way of contrast, when James insists that works are necessary on the last day, he responds to libertinism or antinomianism—the notion that how we live doesn't matter, that grace frees us from any moral obligation. The particular emphases of both Paul and James are crafted to address the circumstances in their churches, and they were not penning systematic theologies. Forming a systematic theology from all of Scripture is right and good, but in doing so we must interpret each piece of literature in its historical and canonical context. All of this is to say

7. See here Chris Bruno, *Paul vs. James: What We've Been Missing in the Faith and Works Debate* (Chicago: Moody, 2019).

that part of the tension we perceive between James and Paul is explained by the situations and circumstances in the churches.

This brings us back to the meaning of "faith" in Paul and James. As noted in the chapter on Paul, he often emphasizes that faith saves, but the faith that saves (cf. Rom. 4:17–25) rests on God's promise in Christ Jesus, just as Abraham trusted that the Lord would give life to his body and to Sarah's womb. True faith as the Reformers emphasized includes *notitia*, *assensus*, and *fiducia*. *Notitia* has to do with what we must *know* to believe, specifically that Jesus was crucified and raised from the dead for the sake of sinners. But knowing such facts isn't enough to bring salvation. One must also assent (*assensus*) to these truths and actually believe them. One may know that there is a vaccine for polio but refuse to believe it. Still even *assensus* isn't enough for salvation; *fiducia* is also required. Perhaps the best word to describe *fiducia* is trust, where one gives oneself to Jesus Christ, where one relies on him for deliverance. For Paul faith involves all three of these realities, and he particularly emphasizes *fiducia*, entrusting oneself to Jesus Christ.

When we examine carefully James 2:14–26, we see that he protests against a view of faith that consists only of *notitia* and *assensus*. This is quite evident as we read the text carefully. James asks in 2:14 if a particular kind of faith saves, a faith that is bereft of works. His answer is emphatically "no," for such faith isn't saving or justifying faith. It is as unreal as pretending to care for a person by saying that we hope they will be clothed and fed while refusing to assist them in any way. Faith shows its reality, its vitality, its authenticity by works. For instance, if one really believes that the polio vaccine is effective, one will take the vaccine. James 2:19 is particularly important in discerning what James is after. Demons are monotheists; they assent to the creed and affirm that there is one God, but they "shudder." In other words, demons lack *fiducia*; they don't entrust themselves to God or rely upon him. James denies justification by faith alone (James 2:24), but when we probe into the context we see that he means that no one is justified by intellectual assent alone, by merely believing the facts about the gospel.

James's insistence on works, then, accords with what the Reformers often said. Justification is by faith alone, but true faith is never alone; it is always accompanied by works, but the works are a fruit of faith, the consequence of faith, the result of faith. Thus, works are not a *basis* of justification but the necessary fruit. When James cites Genesis 15:6 and connects it with Abraham's works and the sacrifice of Isaac, he emphasizes the vitality of faith and the reality of faith. We can only see that faith is a living thing if it shows up in the world, if it makes a difference in one's life. So too with Rahab. Her welcoming of the spies authenticated the reality of her faith. There is a difference between Paul and James with respect to justification as well in that James focuses on the eschatological declaration of righteousness, one that takes the whole frame of faith into view. Paul emphasizes the declaration of righteousness that belongs to one when one believes initially. Still, we don't want to push the difference between Paul and James too far because, for Paul, the declaration of righteousness when one first believes is the eschatological verdict being declared in advance.

One might still say that James and Paul have fundamentally different views of justification since Paul dismisses works altogether, but I will show in chapter 7 that faith alone doesn't rule out works as a fruit of faith in Paul. It should be noted as well that James doesn't see works as a *basis* of justification since believers are still sinners and God demands perfection. James 2:10–13 plays a very important role here. He insists that failing to observe even one part of the law renders one a transgressor so that one would hardly be acquitted in court of murder by claiming that he never committed adultery! Hence, believers should show mercy to others so that they will receive mercy in the judgment. James recognizes that our works can't be the basis of our vindication on the final day, that we need God's mercy and grace to enter into his presence.

Another indication that justification can't be based on works stems from James's discussion on the tongue (James 3:1–12). James declares, "We all stumble in many ways" (James 3:2). We should observe that the word "stumble" (*ptaiō*) here means sin, and James uses the same word in James 2:10 in referring to those who fail to keep every part of the law. It is clear, then, that "stumble" refers to sin or transgression. Nor does James exempt himself from sin in the verse since he uses the first-person plural pronoun. The godly James is among those who "stumble in many ways." Nor is there any exception among any people anywhere because he uses the word "all." No one can claim to be exempt from sin, whether male or female, whether rich or poor, whether educated or uneducated, and whatever one's racial background. James isn't finished but says we all sin "in many ways." He refers to the tongue, so we understand what he means. We don't stumble in a few ways or just occasionally but in many ways. The import of this verse for justification is as follows. Since we all sin regularly, justification can't be *based* on our works. Our works show the reality of our faith, but our works can't be the basis of justification since God demands perfection, and we all sin regularly and often.

Conclusion

We have seen in this chapter that justification isn't a frequent topic in the remaining epistles or in the book of Revelation. Still, the conceptual harmony with Paul's teaching on justification is quite remarkable. In various ways these writers emphasize that salvation is achieved by the cross of Christ, by God's grace, by his calling and election. Forgiveness of sins is a gift granted to those who believe since God is gracious, kind, and merciful. The New Testament doesn't invariably use the term "justification," but the reality it points to is expressed in many ways, and there is harmony in that salvation is ascribed to the Lord. Even James's claim that we are justified by works doesn't contradict Paul's teaching that we are justified by faith alone. Both Paul and James teach that faith saves, but the faith that saves is evidenced by works. Thus, works aren't the basis of justification. Human beings don't and can't save themselves, and thus all glory and praise and honor belong to God for the deliverance human beings receive.

6

Contemporary Challenges

The teaching of justification by faith alone has been challenged throughout history, particularly by Roman Catholics. In this chapter we will take a brief look at two contemporary challenges. Obviously, given the brevity of this book, I am not exploring these matters in detail nor am I considering other notions that are being promoted. I am giving readers a sense, a taste, of these other options. Readers should explore the bibliography at the conclusion of this book for works that examine these issues in more depth. Here I want to chart out a couple of contemporary challenges and provide a response to what they are suggesting. We will look briefly at the apocalyptic view of Paul and then the new perspective on Paul.

Apocalyptic Reading of Paul

The apocalyptic reading of Paul has had a significant effect on Pauline scholarship in recent years with scholars like Ernst Käsemann, Peter Stuhlmacher, J. Christian Beker, J. Louis Martyn, Martinus de Boer, Beverly Gaventa, Douglas Campbell, and others leading the way. The apocalyptic reading emphasizes the sudden irruption into history of God's salvation in Christ Jesus. Typically, it looks skeptically at salvation history paradigms where there is a linear story of promise and fulfillment. Certainly, scholars in the apocalyptic school don't concur on every matter, and it isn't my purpose here to parse out their differences or to even come close to considering all that they say. Instead, I will pick up some elements that are particularly germane to our subject and give an initial response. I should begin by saying that we don't have to choose between salvation history and apocalyptic, for in Scripture we have a both-and instead of an either-or. We don't find a smooth and unbroken story line, but there *is* a story line, *and* the Lord enters history unexpectedly and dramatically to bring salvation.

Douglas Campbell's reading of Paul has provoked interest and response as he rejects what he calls "justification theory."[1] And yet his description of what Reformed interpreters mean by justification has some significant weaknesses and distortions, and most of the scholars he cites in terms of justification theory would not recognize themselves in Campbell's exposition of their views. Actually, Campbell's own reading of Paul is quite unconvincing. For instance, Campbell maintains that much of the content in Romans 1:18–3:20 stems from a Jewish Christian opponent of Paul, and thus Paul disagrees radically with the view of this "teacher" found in these verses. The "teacher," according to Campbell, argues for retributive punishment, but Paul rejects the teacher's view. Campbell defends his view by carefully sorting out what verses in Romans 1:18–3:20 express the teacher's view and what verses represent Paul's perspective. Campbell's argument here is critical for his view since his interpretation of justification depends on his claim that there is no

1. See particularly, Douglas A. Campbell, *The Deliverance of God: An Apocalyptic Rereading of Justification in Paul* (Grand Rapids, MI: Eerdmans, 2009).

retributive judgment in Paul. His reading of Romans 1–3 is quite unlikely since the criteria for segregating what stems from Paul and what comes from the so-called teacher is quite speculative. The novelty of his interpretation calls into question its validity, and very few scholars thus far have endorsed it. I think it is safe to predict that it will have a relatively short shelf life.

Campbell's reading, as noted above, is tied to his notion that there is no retributive judgment in Paul. His Paul is "hyper-Calvinist" in the sense that the Lord has willed (it seems) to shower his benevolence on all. Campbell's Paul is all love and no judgment. Such a reading is certainly a sunny forecast, but it faces a major problem in that Paul often speaks of final judgment, wrath, and people perishing (e.g., Rom. 1:18, 2:5, 8; 3:5; 4:15; 5:9, 6:16, 21, 23; 1 Cor. 1:18; 3:17; 6:9–10; 15:17–18; 2 Cor. 2:15; 3:9; 11:15; Gal. 1:8–9; 5:2, 4, 21; Eph. 2:3; 5:5, 6; Phil. 3:19; Col. 3:5–6; 2 Thess. 1:5–10). Campbell attempts to skirt around such texts, but it is highly doubtful that his proposal will have any long-term influence. We have seen in the history of interpretation similar attempts to cut away the parts of Paul's letters that don't conform to a particular interpretation, and such attempts are now historical curiosities.

Transformative Righteousness

The traditional Protestant view is that righteousness is forensic, but the apocalyptic school understands God's righteousness to be transformative.[2] On this reading believers are not merely declared to be righteous, but they are made righteous in that they are transformed by the saving righteousness of God. Several arguments are presented in defense of this reading.

2. See, e.g., Ernst Käsemann, "The Righteousness of God in Paul," in *New Testament Questions of Today*, trans. W. J. Montague (Philadelphia: Fortress, 1969), 168–82; Peter Stuhlmacher, *Biblical Theology of the New Testament*, trans. and ed. Daniel Bailey and Josten Ådna (Grand Rapids, MI: Eerdmans, 2018), 360–76.

First, "the righteousness of God" (Rom. 1:17) is said to be transformative because it is parallel with "the power of God" (1:16) and "the wrath of God" (1:18). Clearly, God's power and wrath are active in the world and produce an effect. Similarly, God's saving righteousness changes those who believe.

Second, God's righteousness is "revealed" (*apokalyptetai*, Rom. 1:17) and "manifested" (*pephanerōtai*, Rom. 3:21), and these two verbs are apocalyptic, describing the invasion of God's righteousness into history. God's power and transforming grace are unveiled in his saving work.

Third, we read in Romans 5:19, "For as by the one man's disobedience the many were made sinners, so by the one man's obedience the many will be made righteous." The verse is interpreted to say that believers are not merely forensically declared to be in the right but that they are also *made* to be righteous. People are not only declared to be sinners in Adam but also *are* sinners in Adam. If we follow the parallel, just as believers become actual sinners in Adam, so too they actually become righteous in Christ.

Fourth, Romans 6:7 says, "One who has died has been set free from sin." The verb translated "set free" is *dedikaiōtai* from the verb "justify" (*dikaioō*). We have a clear instance where "justify" can't be limited to forensic categories since Romans 6 describes the new life believers live as those who have died and risen with Christ. The translation "set free" confirms that transformation is intended. Those who belong to Christ are now "slaves of righteousness" (Rom. 6:18) so that they live in a way that pleases God.

Fifth, some think the transformative view is correct since justification is ours through the death and resurrection of Christ (Rom. 4:25). Often justification is restricted to Christ's death, and the resurrection is left behind and forgotten. Yet justification doesn't become a reality apart from Christ's death *and* resurrection. The resurrection points to the age to come intervening in the present evil age, to the new life that believers live because God has poured out his grace on his people.

Sixth, a transformative view is supported by the parallel in 2 Corinthians 3:8–9: "the ministry of the Spirit" (3:8) and "the ministry of righteousness" (3:9). The collocation of these two expressions is significant, showing that justification isn't merely forensic since righteousness includes the transforming and liberating work of the Spirit. The Spirit is the Spirit of life, the Spirit that changes, renews, and transforms believers.

Responses to the Transformative View

The arguments for a transformative reading are quite impressive, and they have persuaded many. Still, a forensic reading is more likely. I will not repeat the reasons given in chapter 4 supporting a forensic reading but will take up and respond to the arguments given for the transformative reading.

First, the parallelism that exists in the phrases "the power of God" (Rom. 1:16), "the righteousness of God" (Rom. 1:17), and "the wrath of God" (Rom. 1:18) is striking. Still, we can lurch into a mistake if we conclude that the collocation of these terms demonstrates that God's righteousness is transformative. It makes perfect sense to see all three as divine actions, but it doesn't logically or exegetically follow from this that God's righteousness is transforming. God's righteousness could just as easily denote a divine action by which he declares believers to stand not guilty in his presence, and I have argued in chapter 4 that there is good evidence to support the notion that righteousness has a forensic meaning.

The second argument is rather like the first. The apocalyptic school rightly claims that God's righteousness being "revealed"

(Rom. 1:17) and "manifested" (Rom. 3:21) designates divine activity. Thus, the two verbs signify an apocalyptic and saving activity of God that interpenetrates history. Still, the same objection exists that was made for the first point. Yes, God's righteousness describes his activity that breaks into history. But there is no problem with or contradiction in saying that God's work in the world, his saving righteousness, is a forensic reality. God's righteousness that is revealed and manifested declares sinners to be in the right before him.

Third, Romans 5:19 seems to support a transformative reading since those in Adam are "made sinners" and those in Christ are "made righteous." I observed earlier, however, that the verb "made" (*kathistēmi*) often has the meaning "appoint," which accords with a forensic meaning. Adam and Christ were appointed to be covenant heads for human beings so that human beings are sinners because they are in Adam, and they become righteous if they are in Christ. This is not to deny the actuality and reality of sin or righteousness, but what must be seen is that the forensic comes first and is foundational. Adam and Christ are appointed as our covenant heads, and thus representation precedes reality. In other words, we become sinners since Adam is our representative head, and we become righteous when Christ functions as our covenantal representative. The context, where Adam and Christ are the two representatives for all of humanity, actually supports a forensic reading. The text, then, supports a forensic understanding since the forensic precedes the transformative.

Fourth, Romans 6:7 seems to be a particularly powerful argument for a transformative reading, but several things can be said in reply. It may be the case that the verb *dikaioō* ("justify"), when it is combined with the preposition *apo* ("of" or "from"), has the meaning "freed," but nowhere else does Paul use the verb "justify" with this preposition. Thus, the meaning of the verb in this instance says nothing about what the verb means in other cases. Another important observation should be made. Those who study lexicography know that words have a range of meaning and that in different contexts they may have a different nuance or different meaning. Words don't always have the same meaning, and thus context and the semantic range of a term are fundamental in defining a word. Thus, it is possible that the verb *dikaioō* in Romans 6:7 designates the freedom from sin experienced by those united with Christ. No one disputes, after all, that those who are justified are also transformed. The question before us is whether justification in Paul is forensic or transformative. So even if the verb in Romans 6:7 has a transformative meaning, it hardly follows that this is how Paul typically uses the verb. The difference in meaning in this instance may be accounted for by the added preposition. What I am saying is that one slice doesn't make a pie. We have seen that there are solid grounds for saying that the verb *dikaioō* ("justify") is consistently forensic in Paul, and this one instance here doesn't negate that claim. It should also be noted that the meaning of the verb in Romans 6:7 could be forensic as well. Perhaps Paul is saying that those who have died with Christ are acquitted from sin, and if that is the case, then the forensic reality that is true for believers in Christ is the basis for the transformative.

Fifth, we are rightly reminded from Romans 4:25 that justification is based on both the death and resurrection of Christ. We can think of Romans 5:9–10 as well: on the last day we will be saved from God's wrath and we "shall . . . be saved by his life" (5:10), where the latter clearly refers to the resurrection. Yes, the resurrection power of Christ is ours when we put our trust in him, and we are transformed by his grace, but none of this establishes that justification is transformative. In fact,

Christ's death and resurrection fit well with the notion that righteousness is imputed to us, that our new life is based on both his sacrifice for us and his life that is the basis for our life. The resurrection of Christ certifies that his taking the penalty of sin on our behalf was accepted. If he wasn't raised from the dead, we would have no reason to think that Christ's death removed our sins. Jesus would be another failed messianic figure. Thus, we stand in the right before God based on Jesus's death and resurrection, both his sacrifice and his life.

Sixth, the parallel between "the ministry of the Spirit" and "the ministry of righteousness" in 2 Corinthians 3:8–9 isn't decisive for the transformative view. We shouldn't think that the two expressions mean the same thing simply because they are parallel to one another. The two are closely related but not synonymous. Once again, it is true that those who belong to Christ are also transformed by the Spirit, but it doesn't follow exegetically or logically that the two expressions bear the same meaning. In fact, in 2 Corinthians 3:9 "the ministry of righteousness" is contrasted with "the ministry of condemnation." In this case, righteousness and condemnation are clearly contrasted with each other and function as antonyms. Hence, it would follow, if the transformative view were correct, that "righteousness" means "make righteous" and "condemnation" means "make wicked." But this seems quite improbable since God doesn't make people wicked but declares those who are unrighteous to be wicked. It is much more likely that the nouns "righteousness" and "condemnation" are both forensic. Those under the Mosaic covenant and ministry are declared to be wicked while those in the new covenant are declared to be in the right.

The apocalyptic view rightly emphasizes the freedom of God's grace and the irruption of that grace in history in unexpected and surprising ways. God's grace stands in radical contrast to the sinfulness and wickedness of human beings. Even Campbell shares an important insight and truth in featuring the wonder of divine benevolence, though he pushes that theme too far and eliminates retributive judgment from Paul's theology. The apocalyptic school also fails to persuade in drawing the conclusion that righteousness in Paul is a transformative reality. The lexical evidence (which was presented in chapter 4) indicates that the forensic view is more persuasive, and the instances they use to defend their reading can be explained in other ways that are more satisfactory.

New Perspective on Paul

The so-called new perspective on Paul isn't very new anymore.[3] We could say that it was launched in 1977 with the publication of E. P. Sanders's book *Paul and Palestinian Judaism*, and that was more than forty years ago.[4] In many ways Krister Stendahl (who preceded Sanders) anticipated or perhaps served as the inspiration for the new perspective. Actually, there isn't one new perspective but multiple new perspectives since all the adherents don't stand in the same place. Probably the two most prominent advocates are James D. G. Dunn[5] and N. T. Wright,[6] with Wright holding pride of place at least in evangelical circles. Once again, the discussion here can't delve into technical matters but rather skims over the top. There are some things that have already been discussed such as works of the law, and thus I won't

3. See the stimulating and groundbreaking work by John M. G. Barclay, *Paul and the Gift* (Grand Rapids, MI: Eerdmans, 2015), which challenges the new perspective at a number of levels.

4. E. P. Sanders, *Paul and Palestinian Judaism: A Comparison of Patterns of Religion* (Minneapolis: Fortress, 1977).

5. E.g., James D. G. Dunn, "The New Perspective on Paul," *Bulletin of the John Rylands University Library of Manchester* 65 (1983): 95–122.

6. N. T. Wright, *Justification: God's Plan and Paul's Vision* (Downers Grove, IL: IVP Academic, 2009).

replicate what was said previously, but here some prominent and important notions of the new perspective will be discussed.

The new perspective has emphasized the sociological character of Paul's theology. Thus, Paul did not criticize fellow Jews, according to the new perspective, for their disobedience or legalism. If one follows Sanders, legalism wasn't even an issue in Judaism since Second Temple Jews propounded a theology of grace—what Sanders calls "covenantal nomism." On this understanding, the Lord entered into a covenant with Israel by grace, and the keeping of the law was a response to God's grace. Scholars like Dunn and Wright think that Sanders has rightly explained the nature of Judaism during the Second Temple period. Thus, Paul's complaint, according to Dunn and Wright, wasn't that the law could not be disobeyed or that people were guilty of works-righteousness. Instead, they claim that the problem with the Jews of Paul's day is that they used the law to exclude the Gentiles from the people of God. Their defect wasn't legalism but nationalism: it wasn't works righteousness but ethnocentrism. The ethnocentrism of the Jews manifested itself in the exclusion of Gentiles, and thus they centered on circumcision, Sabbath, and food laws—laws that segregated Jews from the Gentiles. The Jews weren't obsessed with trying to earn God's favor but used boundary markers to fence off the people of God, thus shutting off the Gentiles from a relationship with God. If the fundamental problem was Jewish exclusivism, we understand why Wright claims that justification is fundamentally about ecclesiology instead of soteriology, about covenant membership instead of covenant salvation.

We need to delve further into what is meant by covenant nomism since many new perspective adherents use this as a foundation for their understanding of Paul. Sanders's book has its virtues. For instance, he helps us avoid a caricature of Judaism where one sees legalism everywhere and all the time. There is a virtue in hearing Judaism with its own voice instead of imposing on it a narrative of our own making. Still, a number of scholars have raised significant objections about Sanders's reading of Second Temple Jewish sources.[7] He was probably too eager to find an undifferentiated narrative in the sources when the reality was more complex. When we look at the texts, Second Temple Judaism can't be neatly plotted along one line; there are instances where the law isn't clearly placed within a covenant framework, where any emphasis on grace is virtually absent. Also, there are indications that at least some Jews tried to secure their righteousness by their obedience. And we see this in the New Testament as well.

In the story of the Pharisee and the tax collector (Luke 18:9–14), the Pharisee commends himself to God based on his extraordinary obedience. It would be passing strange for Jesus to speak against such "legalism" if it didn't even exist, if no one struggled with such matters, if it was not a common problem. We find something quite similar in Paul. He counters those who think about their obedience to the law as one thinks about getting paid for one's work (Rom. 4:4). The illustration clearly shows that Paul speaks against those who think their obedience to the law warranted a reward.

The alleged emphasis on ethnocentricism is tied up with works of the law, and I argued previously that works of the

7. E.g., Friedrich Avemarie, *Tora und Bund Tora und Leben: Untersuchungen zur Heilsbedeutung der Tora in der frühen rabbinischen Literatur*, Texte und Studien zum antiken Judentum 55 (Tübingen: Mohr Siebeck, 1996); Simon Gathercole, *Where Is Boasting? Early Jewish Soteriology and Paul's Response in Romans 1–5* (Grand Rapids, MI: Eerdmans, 2003); Andrew A. Das, *Paul, the Law, and the Covenant* (Peabody, MA: Hendrickson, 1998); Mark A. Elliott, *The Survivors of Israel: A Reconsideration of the Theology of Pre-Christian Judaism* (Grand Rapids, MI: Eerdmans, 2000); D. A. Carson, Peter T. O'Brien, and Mark A. Seifrid, eds., *The Complexities of Second Temple Judaism*, vol. 1 of *Justification and Variegated Nomism* (Grand Rapids, MI: Baker Academic, 2001).

law can't be restricted to the badges of the law, that the entire law is in view, and thus a focus on boundary markers can't be pinned on the use of the term "works of the law." Wright, however, makes the point that justification is fundamentally about covenant membership, about whom fellow believers can eat with.[8] When we look at the verb "justify," however, it seems that this interpretation is skewed. Justification is fundamentally vertical, having to do with one's relationship with God. Certainly, justification has implications for covenant membership and whom one has fellowship with at table, but the focus is soteriological and vertical, speaking to one's relationship with God.

That justification is fundamentally vertical is clear from looking at the use of the term. For instance, when we are told that those who keep the law "will be justified" (Rom. 2:13), this clearly denotes those who are right *before God* and doesn't speak directly to the issue of covenant membership. Similarly, those who don't do the works of the law won't be justified in God's presence (Rom. 3:20, 28; Gal. 2:16). The words "in his sight" (Rom. 3:20) indicate that one's relation with God is in view. Abraham's works don't meet the standard in terms of being justified "before God" (Rom. 4:2), and he was counted as righteous in his relationship to God (Rom. 4:3). The reference to God counting or not counting someone as righteous underscores one's relation to God (Rom. 4:3, 6, 9, 11, 22; Gal. 3:6). So, too, God justifying the ungodly (Rom. 4:5) certainly focuses on one's relationship with God, not one's fellowship with church members. This fits with the claim that those who are "justified by faith . . . have peace with God" (Rom. 5:1), not first and foremost peace with one another. Justification means

8. N. T. Wright, *What Saint Paul Really Said: Was Paul of Tarsus the Real Founder of Christianity?* (Grand Rapids, MI: Eerdmans, 1997), 125; Wright, *Justification*, 132–34.

that one stands in the right in God's law court since no one can bring any charge of condemnation against God's chosen ones (Rom. 8:33).

In 2 Corinthians 5:21 Christ died so that believers would enjoy the righteousness of God, and thus righteousness is based on atonement (cf. Rom. 3:21–26), showing that a relation with God is intended. The salvific character seems clear in Galatians 2:21 where, if righteousness comes from the law, Christ died for nothing. Once again, the atoning work of Christ is connected to justification. Along the same lines, those who try to be justified by the law are cut off from Christ (Gal. 5:4). Those who try to establish their own righteous don't submit themselves to God's righteousness (Rom. 10:3). Certainly, they are removed from the church as well, yet Paul doesn't emphasize the ecclesiological dimension but the soteriological.

The soteriological cast of righteousness and justification is clear since it is related to redemption (Rom. 3:24; 1 Cor. 1:30); forgiveness (Rom. 4:25; 5:16); salvation through Christ's blood (Rom. 5:9; 10:10; Titus 3:5); reconciliation (Rom. 5:10); life of the age to come (Rom. 5:18; Gal. 3:11, 21); predestination, calling, and glorification (Rom. 8:30); being washed and sanctified (1 Cor. 6:11; cf. also 1 Cor. 1:30); and grace (Gal. 5:4; Titus 3:7). All of this fits with Philippians 3:9 that refers to "righteousness from God" instead of righteousness from observance of the law. The evidence above is actually quite overwhelming. The soteriological nature of justification stands out in virtually every reference, and it is abundantly clear that it has to do with one's relationship to God. At the same time, virtually nothing is said about one's horizontal relationship with other believers. Certainly, justification speaks to our relation with fellow believers, but the primary orbit of the term itself is soteriology.

Imputation

The scholar who has questioned imputation most sharply is N. T. Wright. Two quotes from him make his view clear: "If Paul uses the language of the law court, it makes no sense whatever to say that the judge imputes, imparts, bequeaths, conveys or otherwise transfers his righteousness either to the plaintiff or the defendant."[9] "When the judge in the lawcourt justifies someone, he does not give that person his own particular 'righteousness.' He *creates* the status the vindicated defendant now possesses, by an act of *declaration*, a 'speech-act' in our contemporary jargon."[10] Wright emphasizes that judges never give their righteousness to defendants. Judges don't hand over their righteousness to others; they decide and determine and pronounce on the righteousness or guilt of defendants.

Wright is correct in his observations about how judges behave in courtrooms. They never give their righteousness to defendants, and there is no provision or category in the law for them to do so. We would be outraged if they did so, wondering how they would dare to presume that they could give their righteousness to a defendant. But Wright makes a fundamental mistake from the outset. He assumes that God's role as a judge accords exactly with what happens in human courtrooms, but we can't constrain the courtroom metaphor by what typically happens in human courts. We have to allow biblical writers to use the metaphor in the way they choose. In other words, Wright is correct in saying that judges never give their righteousness to defendants in human courtrooms, but he fails to

9. Wright, *What Saint Paul Really Said*, 98. He goes on to say, "To imagine the defendant somehow receiving the judge's righteousness is simply a category mistake. That is not how language works" (98).

10. Wright, *Justification*, 69 (emphasis in original). "*But the righteousness they have will not be God's own righteousness*. That makes no sense at all. God's own righteousness is his covenant faithfulness. . . . But God's righteousness remains his own property." Wright, *What Saint Paul Really Said*, 99 (emphasis in original).

see that when a human being stands before God this is not an ordinary courtroom. What happens in human courtrooms can't dictate the relationship of people to God or to how God adjudicates affairs in his courtroom. Further, the wonder of the gospel is that God grants us his righteousness as we are united by faith to Jesus the Christ. We would not expect such a state of affairs, and it would never happen in a human courtroom. But there is no other situation in which God out of love sends his Son (who comes in love) to redeem his people so that the judgment they deserve because of sin is visited on the Son.

There is no need to rehearse again the texts cited earlier in defense of imputation, but we will return to one text momentarily. If we look at broader categories, Wright's rejection of imputation can be assigned to an inadequate understanding of union with Christ. When believers are united with Christ, everything that Christ is becomes theirs. His righteousness is given to us because we are "in" him, because we are united to him by faith. Thus, imputation doesn't simply hang on one or two texts but accords with the broader parameters of Paul's theology, with the affirmation that believers belong to Christ by faith.

Wright maintains that 2 Corinthians 5:21 doesn't support imputation.[11] He says the plural "we" in 2 Corinthians 5:21 refers to the apostle and his ministry, given the use of the other first-person plural verbs in context, and thus the verse isn't referring to all believers. Furthermore, the verb "become" in the verse should be understood as a process. But both of these points can be disputed. It is true that most of the first-person plurals in 2 Corinthians 5 refer to Paul, but Paul easily slides between believers and himself in using first-person pronouns. He uses pronouns fluidly and rather unsystematically so that

11. Wright, *What Saint Paul Really Said*, 104–5; Wright, *Justification*, 159–64.

we should not press the first-person plurals as if they all refer to Paul and only to Paul. After all, Paul isn't writing a technical treatise but a letter, and thus when he speaks of Christ who "reconciled us to himself" (2 Cor. 5:18), he probably includes all believers in the words "us." Even if that doesn't convince, 2 Corinthians 5:21 represents a kind of confessional statement about the benefits of the cross, and it is unlikely that it should be restricted to Paul alone. Such confessional-type statements are peppered throughout Paul's letters, and they are particularly prominent when the cross is the subject matter. By definition confessional statements include all Christians.

When we consider the plural verb "become" (*genōmetha*) in 2 Corinthians 5:21, it doesn't clearly indicate, contrary to Wright, a process. In fact, the verb is often equivalent to the verb "to be" (*eimi*). One of the most careful Greek grammarians of our time, Murray Harris, thinks that the verb "become" doesn't indicate a process in this text.[12] Harris goes on to say that "it is not inappropriate to perceive in this verse a double imputation: sin was reckoned to Christ's account (v. 21a), so that righteousness is reckoned to our account (v. 21b)."[13] Indeed, "As a result of God imputing to Christ something extrinsic to him, namely sin, believers have something imputed to them that was extrinsic to them, namely righteousness."[14] We understand why Wright hesitates to affirm imputation, but when we understand the scriptural teaching on union with Christ, the uniqueness of his death for sinners, and the particular texts in question, we have good grounds for saying that this conception is faithful to Paul.

12. Murray J. Harris, *The Second Epistle to the Corinthians: A Commentary on the Greek Text*, The New International Greek Testament Commentary (Grand Rapids, MI: Eerdmans, 2005), 455.
13. Harris, *The Second Epistle to the Corinthians*, 455.
14. Harris, *The Second Epistle to the Corinthians*, 455.

Nor is it convincing to say that imputation is a legal fiction as many have alleged throughout history. It isn't a fabrication because we really do stand in the right before a holy God. Christ's righteousness is truly ours and is truly credited to our account. Perhaps some think it is a legal fiction because they are conceiving of what happens in a typical courtroom, but here we have a righteousness counted to people by the living God, and righteousness is really theirs because they are united to Christ by faith.

Conclusion

In this chapter we considered some features of the new perspective on Paul and apocalyptic readings of Paul. The apocalyptic school rightly sees that God dramatically enters history in a surprising and unexpected way in Jesus Christ, but it goes astray in understanding God's righteousness to be transformative instead of forensic. We also saw that Douglas Campbell strays in denying God's retributive justice since final judgment is a common teaching in Paul. The new perspective has rightly reminded us of the Jew-Gentile dimension of Paul's gospel and the social realities that are sometimes missed by those in the Reformed tradition. But it also goes astray when it claims that there is no polemic against works-righteousness in Paul, when it says that justification is horizontal rather than vertical, and when it denies imputation. We want to be open to and learn from new voices, but we must also recognize that historic teachings have stood the test of time for a reason.

7

Justification and Systematic Theology

The focus in this book has been the unpacking of particular texts relative to justification, but it also pays to consider at least briefly justification and its relationship to other realities. In other words, it will prove helpful to consider justification in terms of systematic theology, since in systematic theology all that Scripture teaches is put together coherently and reasonably.

Systematics is rightly viewed as the culmination of exegesis, biblical theology, historical theology, and philosophy. In some circles systematics is scorned as a discipline, particularly among some who focus on being biblical. Still, such a stance is shortsighted and counterproductive since we all operate, whether we know it or not, with a systematic theology. The issue is whether our system is truly biblical and comprehensive. Of course, no sane person claims to have all the answers, and there is no perfect systematic theology in this world since there are no perfect systematicians. Furthermore, the Scriptures don't claim to give us fully comprehensive answers, though we are given what we need to know (they are sufficient) for salvation and sanctification. Nevertheless, systematic theology is a noble and necessary task.

As is the case throughout this book, I am just touching on some issues in this chapter, priming the pump so that readers can pursue these matters in more depth elsewhere. Since most of the issues pertain to Pauline theology, I will concentrate on his contribution in particular. In this last chapter I will consider two matters: (1) the relationship between justification and other salvific realities like union with Christ, redemption, reconciliation, and so on; and (2) discussion of justification by works.

Justification and Other Salvific Realities

Paul often speaks of being "in Christ," and virtually all agree that union with Christ plays a significant role in this theology.[1] The soteriological benefits of being in Christ reveal a high Christology, in which Christ is the eternal Word/Son from the Father who took on flesh for us and for our salvation (John 1:14–18). We have already seen in Romans 5:12–19 (cf. 1 Cor. 15:21–22) that people are either in Adam or in Christ. We need to be careful since the phrase "in Christ" is used in a variety of ways and doesn't necessarily denote union with him.[2] I have already argued, however, that one of the key texts on justification (2 Cor. 5:21) should be understood in terms of union with Christ, and this is supported by the Adam and Christ contrast that we find in Romans 5, where both Adam and Christ are covenant representatives, covenant heads.

1. For a useful study of the "in Christ" formula in Paul, see Mark A. Seifrid, "In Christ," in *Dictionary of Paul and His Letters*, ed. G. F. Hawthorne and R. P. Martin (Downers Grove, IL: InterVarsity Press, 1993), 433–36.

2. See Constantine R. Campbell, *Paul and Union with Christ: An Exegetical and Theological Study* (Grand Rapids, MI: Zondervan Academic, 2012). For weaknesses in Campbell's book, see the brilliant review by Mark Seifrid in *Themelios* 38, no. 2 (2013): 262–64, https://www.thegospelcoalition.org/themelios/review/paul-and-union-with-christ-an-exegetical-and-theological-study.

Many soteriological realities are ours in Christ: redemption (Rom. 3:24), life and resurrection (Rom. 6:11, 23; 8:2; Eph. 2:6; 2 Tim. 1:1), freedom from condemnation (Rom. 8:1), sanctification (1 Cor. 1:2), election (1 Cor. 1:28–30; Eph. 1:4; 2 Tim. 1:9), new creation (2 Cor. 5:17; Eph. 2:10), reconciliation (2 Cor. 5:19), the blessing of Abraham (Gal. 3:14), every spiritual blessing (Eph. 1:3), salvation (2 Tim. 2:10), grace (1 Cor. 1:4), and *justification* (Gal. 2:17). John Calvin says that union with Christ has "the highest degree of importance" if we are to understand justification correctly.[3] He also remarks, "We must understand that as long as Christ remains outside of us, and we are separated from him, all that he has suffered and done for the salvation of the human race remains useless and of no value for us. . . . All that he possesses is nothing to us until we grow into one body with him."[4] Robert Letham declares, "Union with Christ is right at the center of the Christian doctrine of salvation. The whole of our relationship with God can be summed up in such terms."[5]

It is quite remarkable how so many elements of salvation in Paul are connected to union with Christ. It seems fair to say that union with Christ is the overarching category so that justification, redemption, reconciliation, election, and more are all in Christ. I am not contending that union with Christ is the center of Paul's thought or the most important theme. Union with Christ is the broader category and justification fits under that umbrella. This is not to say that justification is of minor importance since the question of being right with God is fundamental and foundational. Still, it seems that union with Christ stands

3. John Calvin, *Institutes of the Christian Religion*, ed. John T. McNeill, trans. Ford Lewis Battles, 2 vols. (Philadelphia: Westminster, 1960), 3.11.10 (1:737).

4. Calvin, *Institutes*, 3.1.1 (1:537).

5. Robert Letham, *Union with Christ in Scripture, History, and Theology* (Phillipsburg, NJ: P&R, 2011), 1. Thanks to Oren Martin for these citations from Calvin and Letham.

out as being distinct from salvation, new creation, justification, redemption, reconciliation, and the rest. All those other salvific blessings come to human beings when they are united to Christ by faith. It seems, then, that union with Christ is more inclusive, when we talk about Paul's theology, than justification, reconciliation, or any of the other saving realities.

How should we understand the relationship of justification to other salvific blessings, such as regeneration, redemption, reconciliation, sanctification, adoption, new creation, election, calling, and eternal life? Is justification more important than these other designations of salvation? Should we consider it to be fundamental or foundational or in some sense prior? These questions are complex, and there is space here only for suggestive comments.

I suggest that there is a sense in which all of these different ways of describing our salvation are equal, and at the same time there is a sense in which justification is fundamental. This needs to be explained and unpacked briefly.

On the one hand, the various perspectives of salvation are on the same level because they describe with different images God's saving work granted to Christians. For instance, *salvation* and *redemption* both describe how God has rescued his people, delivering them from sin, death, and Satan. Such a deliverance doesn't depend on the goodness or righteousness of human beings but is rooted in the grace of God. We can also think of *reconciliation* or enjoying peace with God. Paul emphasizes that reconciliation is initiated and accomplished by God (Rom. 5:1, 10; 2 Cor. 5:18–21; Eph. 2:11–22). Human beings are God's enemies (Rom. 5:10) resisting his will and his ways, but the Lord takes the initiative to reconcile us to himself so that we enjoy peace with him. *Sanctification*, which has to do with being placed in the realm of the holy, is also the work of the Lord so that sanctification is ours in Christ Jesus (1 Cor. 1:30; 6:11).

Similarly, *regeneration* or being born again captures the new life bestowed on believers, and as a consequence we are adopted and become children of God. No one chooses to be born, and similarly the new birth represents God's gracious and supernatural work. To put it another way, those who are born again enjoy eternal life, the life of the age to come. *New creation* also lifts our eyes to the Lord's work (2 Cor. 5:17; Gal. 6:15). God created the physical world by his word (e.g., Gen. 1:3; Ps. 33:6), and by his word and work he inaugurates the new creation. *Election* and *calling* also should be noted since God chooses who will be saved apart from human works and before we are born (Rom. 9:11; Eph. 1:4). And calling, which takes place in history as the gospel is proclaimed (2 Thess. 2:14), is effectual (cf. Rom. 8:30; 1 Cor. 1:23–24, 26), and thus the term can't be equated with an invitation to be saved. Instead, God's calling creates life.

What stands out with all these different images is that God saves his people. He redeems, reconciles, regenerates, saves, sanctifies, adopts, elects, and calls. In this sense justification accords with the various salvific metaphors that Paul uses. In every instance salvation is of the Lord. There is no sense in any instance that human works or ability account for God's saving power. Instead, the focus is entirely on the grace of God that is poured out in his great mercy on his people. The parallels are instructive because in one sense the emphasis on justification being God's work isn't novel or distinctive. Justification is simply another way of saying that God is the one who saves, that salvation can't be ascribed to the human subject, to human effort and virtue. Some theologians might give the impression that justification is all there is to say about soteriology, as if it stands out in splendid isolation from the other metaphors for salvation. The reality is remarkably different. Indeed, it is striking how all the metaphors emphasize that salvation is transcendent, heavenly—a divine work. Indeed, if justification stood apart from the other metaphors in emphasizing God's work in saving his people, it would sit awkwardly with the rest of the New Testament. In reality it fits with the larger picture and landscape so that we recognize that salvation is of the Lord.

On the other hand, justification is particularly prominent since Paul contrasts justification so often with condemnation. We have seen that Paul often emphasizes that justification is by faith instead of by works. Here justification is closest to salvation since it is also asserted that salvation is by faith. We don't have the same emphasis on faith when it comes to sanctification, redemption, and reconciliation, though this observation should not be pressed too far because faith isn't absent in such instances. Still, justification poses more sharply the congruence, or lack thereof, of the human and divine roles when it comes to a relationship with God. Thus, we are pressed to discern theologically and practically what it means to say that justification is by faith instead of by works—a theme particularly emphasized by Paul.

Christendom has been divided over what role human beings play in terms of justification, and thus it has naturally come to the forefront from the time of the Reformation. In one sense, justification doesn't play a more decisive role than, say, redemption or reconciliation, since in every case salvation is the Lord's work. But on the other hand, justification compels us to discern the contribution of the human being in terms of being right with God. Is our work or God's work foundational in our salvation? I have argued in this book that the Reformed construal is on target, preserving what we see in other soteric realities—namely, that salvation is of the Lord. Humans don't merit, earn, or achieve their salvation—even their faith is a gift.

Justification has a fundamental role in another sense in that it explains the basis on which the Lord forgives and declares sinners to stand in the right before him. Once again there is a sense in which that statement is too simple since redemption, reconciliation, and sanctification are based on the cross. Still, when it comes to justification the process is explicated with a unique clarity. We have seen that human beings don't stand in the right before a holy God because of their sin. Since God is perfectly and infinitely holy, no sinner has any warrant for life. Instead, all deserve to be condemned and judged for their wickedness. Justification has to do with the language of the law court and considers in a particular way how one may stand before the divine judge and receive the verdict "not guilty." We see in a number of texts (e.g., Rom. 3:21–26; Gal. 3:13; 2 Cor. 5:21; 1 Pet. 2:24; 3:18) that Jesus as the Son of God takes the place of sinners, that the curse and judgment sinners deserve is taken by him. We don't have an instance of an angry God forcing his Son to die for sinners. Instead, God in his love sent his Son who came in love to give himself for sinners. We have an example here of the important Trinitarian doctrine of inseparable operations.[6] The Father and the Son don't work against each other but in concert and in harmony, and, of course, the Holy Spirit fits with this picture (cf. 1 Cor. 6:11), applying the great work of salvation to our hearts.

6. The doctrine grew out of an entailment of the doctrine of the unity and simplicity of God, as Augustine puts it in *The Trinity*, vol. 45 in *The Fathers of the Church: A New Translation,* trans. Stephen McKenna (Washington DC: The Catholic University of America, 1963), 11: "the Father, the Son, and the Holy Spirit, as they are inseparable, so they work inseparably." For more, see Adonis Vidu, *The Same God Who Works All Things: Inseparable Operations in Trinitarian Theology* (Grand Rapids, MI: Eerdmans, 2021).

Justification impresses on us in a distinctive way the holiness and love of God. He is both "just and the justifier of the one who has faith in Jesus" (Rom. 3:26). Such is the work of the cross where the love and holiness of God meet, where wrath is satisfied and mercy is displayed, where God's judging righteousness and saving righteousness are both expressed, where justice is achieved and grace is received. The legal character of justification seems cold to some, but such a response betrays a serious misunderstanding since the legal verdict is an expression of love. Those who scan Christian hymns and choruses will readily see that the death of Christ on the cross by which he took the penalty sinners deserve has led believers to praise God with joy. The legal act isn't separated from a vibrant life but has filled believers with a joy that bursts all bounds.

Since justification articulates in a precise way how God vindicates and acquits sinners—based on the penal substitutionary death of his Son—it plays a unique role in unpacking the logic of our salvation, reminding us that neither the love of God nor the holiness of God is compromised in the cross. The legal act isn't cold or unfeeling because it communicates to us powerfully the nature of God, showing God's great love in that he has satisfied his own justice (Rom. 3:24–26; Gal. 3:13). It is not, of course, as if there is a law outside of God to which he had to conform. God himself is holy so that forgiving sin without satisfying his justice would violate his character, his very being, his "Godness." Still, at the end of the day, God's attributes can't be played against one another, and thus God's love and justice meet at the cross, and sinners are declared to be in the right when they put their faith in Jesus. At the same time, as we have seen, we can't boast of our faith since that, too, is a mysterious gift of God given to us in accord with his own wise purposes and wondrous love.

Justification by Works

In chapter 5 we considered justification by works in James, arguing that works are the fruit of faith, and that James's conception of faith, even faith alone, doesn't contradict the Pauline view. James doesn't see works as the basis or foundation of faith but as the evidence or fruit of faith. At the same time, we saw in chapter 4 that Paul teaches that believers are justified by faith alone, and such faith stands in contrast to works of the law in particular and to works generally as well. But here we need to examine the other side of the issue and consider whether works play any role, according to Paul, in receiving the final reward.

Before we look at Paul, one text in the Old Testament should be considered, namely, Psalm 62. The psalm is most interesting since it repeatedly emphasizes that salvation comes from God alone.

> For God alone my soul waits in silence;
>   from him comes my salvation.
> He alone is my rock and my salvation,
>   my fortress; I shall not be greatly shaken. (Ps. 62:1–2)

Salvation being from God alone fits with the notion that we are saved by faith alone, since faith puts its trust in the only one who can deliver us. In Psalm 62:5–7 the psalmist again looks to God alone for help:

> For God alone, O my soul, wait in silence,
>   for my hope is from him.
> He only is my rock and my salvation,
>   my fortress; I shall not be shaken.
> On God rests my salvation and my glory;
>   my mighty rock, my refuge is God.

Immediately after this, readers are exhorted to "trust in him at all times" (Ps. 62:8). Here we see the explicit connection between salvation being in God alone and the call to put all one's trust and faith in him. The psalm concludes, however, on an astonishing note:

> For you will render to a man
> according to his work. (Ps. 62:12)

The notion that we are rewarded according to our works seems to come from nowhere in the psalm since the emphasis throughout has been relying on God alone, on trusting in him as one's rock, fortress, and deliverer. The correlation between trusting in God alone and being judged by works, however, is most instructive, for it shows that those who trust in God alone live in a way that pleases God. Relying only on God leads to a life of goodness, a life that is characterized by works that are pleasing to God. Thus, the psalm leads us to the conclusion that faith is the root and good works are the fruit, that good works are the consequence of faith, a result that follows if we trust in God alone.

This brings us to Paul and his understanding of works. I have already argued that "works" and "works of the law" cannot and do not justify according to Paul's theology. The argument being made here is that Paul, like James, believed that works were necessary for justification and eternal life, and that such a statement doesn't contradict Paul's teaching that justification is by faith. The reason this is the case is because Paul, in agreement with James, did not think such works are the *basis* of justification. They are, rather, the necessary fruit and evidence of justification. The words *necessary evidence* are crucial.

Many, when they hear that works are necessary, slide over to the idea that works are the necessary basis, and then they think that we either have a contradiction in Paul's thought or that the Pauline gospel is being denied. But neither of these conclusions should be admitted. Paul clearly and repeatedly teaches that faith saves instead of works. Works can't justify since God demands perfection, and thus justification only comes from being united with Jesus Christ as the crucified and risen one because he has borne the punishment we deserved at the cross. At the same time Paul also affirms that good works are necessary. To say that works are a necessary evidence of salvation is a legitimate theological deduction since there is every reason to believe that Paul is a coherent thinker. More important, the Scriptures are God's inspired word, and thus no contradiction can be present since they are the perfect rule for faith and practice. Further, some exegetical evidence will be presented below supporting the notion that works are a necessary evidence.

Paul teaches that judgment according to works is coming on the last day (Rom. 2:6–10) so that those who indulge in evil will face God's wrath and experience unending distress and anguish (Rom. 2:8–9). Those who are Satan's servants will be assessed by their works on the final day (2 Cor. 11:15). Some who profess to belong to God actually deny him by the works they perform (Titus 1:16). Alexander the coppersmith belongs in this category, and he will face judgment according to his works as one who opposed Paul (2 Tim. 4:14).

The importance of good works is also evident in Paul since believers should be "zealous for good works" (Titus 2:14), put off "the works of darkness" (Rom. 13:12), "abound in every good work" (2 Cor. 9:8), refuse to participate "in the unfruitful works of darkness" (Eph. 5:11), "be rich in good works" (1 Tim. 6:18), be "equipped/ready for every good work" (2 Tim. 3:17; Titus 3:1), show their godliness in "good works" (1 Tim. 2:10), have "a reputation for good works" (1 Tim.

5:10), be an example of "good works" (Titus 2:7), and "devote themselves to good works" (Titus 3:8, 14). The many positive references to good works are quite remarkable, especially since Paul emphasizes so often, as we have seen, that believers are not justified by works!

In Romans 2:13 Paul declares that "the doers of the law . . . will be justified." Some take this statement to be hypothetical, but that is doubtful. In Romans 2:6–10 Paul affirms that every person is rewarded by God according to his works, and Paul gives no indication that he speaks hypothetically. "Eternal life" belongs to those who patiently do what is good (Rom. 2:7), and they will experience on the last day "glory and honor and peace" (Rom. 2:10). We discover in Romans 2:26 that the one who "keeps the precepts of the law," even if he is uncircumcised, is considered to be circumcised. In other words, he is counted as one of the covenant people, as a member of the people of God. Such a one is a true Jew and is truly circumcised (Rom. 2:29). And in this very verse we see with clarity that the discussion is not hypothetical because the one who keeps the law—who is a true Jew and is truly circumcised—does so "by the Spirit," and his "praise," that is, his final reward, is from God. The obedience isn't hypothetical but actual since it is the work of the Holy Spirit, representing the transformation accomplished by God's Spirit in the lives of those who belong to Christ.

We should note the logic that underscores the call for good works. For instance, the zeal for good works in Titus 2:14 is a consequence of Christ's redemptive work. The obedience that marks the life of Christians isn't autonomous or self-generated or humanly achievable. Instead, it comes from one who has received the Spirit by faith (Rom. 8:9; Gal. 3:1–5, 14). We saw this clearly in Romans 2:26–29, which we discussed above. The obedience of Gentile Christians is the work of the Spirit, and the Spirit is given to those who have new life, to those who have confessed their sins and their failure to please God. So once again we see that obedience is a result and consequence of the Spirit's work. The work of the Spirit is no hypothesis but a supernatural reality that can't be attributed to the strength of human beings. Thus, Paul isn't talking about works that merit salvation or are the basis of salvation. The works are the effect of the Spirit's energy in a person's life, showing that a person is transformed and made new.

We also see the necessity of works in Galatians 5:21, where Paul declares that those who practice the works of the flesh (Gal. 5:19–21) "will not inherit the kingdom of God." Nothing could be clearer. Those who practice evil will be excluded from God's eschatological kingdom, while those who do what is good will receive the eschatological reward. This fits with Galatians 6:8: "For the one who sows to his own flesh will from the flesh reap corruption, but the one who sows to the Spirit will from the Spirit reap eternal life." Corruption stands in contrast to eternal life, showing that one's eternal destiny is in view. And those who "sow" to the flesh—to the old Adam, to the sin principle—will experience eschatological destruction, while those who sow to the Spirit will harvest the life of the age to come.

We can say that those who sow to the Spirit only do so by the power of the Holy Spirit. Human beings can't depend on their own resources but lean on the Spirit to produce righteousness. In the same letter where Paul affirms that righteousness doesn't come through the works of the law, he insists that one must live a new way to obtain life in the age to come. But such a new way of life comes from the Spirit, and thus Paul says that believers must "walk by the Spirit" (Gal. 5:16), be "led by the Spirit" (Gal. 5:18), and "live by the Spirit" or "keep in step with the Spirit" (Gal. 5:25). Thus, any good that is done by believers is "the fruit of the Spirit" (Gal. 5:22). The obedience isn't perfect but it is remarkable and supernatural. Those who are right with God by faith and not by their works demonstrate their new life since the Spirit who is granted to them by faith transforms them.

We see something similar in 1 Corinthians 6:1–11 where the Corinthians are reproved for quarreling over civil matters, for asserting their legal rights instead of preferring their neighbors. They are actually engaging in evil (*adikeite*, 1 Cor. 6:8), and those who are unrighteous (*adikoi*) will not inherit God's kingdom (1 Cor. 6:9). They are in danger of being "deceived" (1 Cor. 6:9), apparently concluding that their behavior at court was rather inconsequential, but Paul says their behavior should be classed with adultery, homosexuality, stealing, abusive speech, and idolatry (1 Cor. 6:9–10). In their lust for money evident in their lawsuits, they should probably be placed among the "greedy" (1 Cor. 6:10), and thus their behavior, if it continued, could disqualify them from the kingdom. Paul shakes them back to reality, reminding them that they have been cleansed in baptism, placed in the realm of the holy, and declared to be right in Christ and by the Spirit (1 Cor. 6:11). The behavior demanded does not and cannot merit the kingdom; their place in the kingdom finds its roots in their washing, definitive sanctification, and justification. Still, their obedience verifies and authenticates their new life in Christ, revealing that they are truly new.

A remarkable verse is Philippians 2:12 where the Philippians are reminded of their obedience (*hypēkoustate*) and then, in a most astonishing statement for Paul, told to accomplish or work out (*katergazesthe*) their salvation! The verse seems to be a tribute to human autonomy and virtue, but Paul grounds and gives the foundation for 2:12 in 2:13: "For it is God who works in you, both to will and to work for his good pleasure." Yes, good works are necessary for salvation, but these works are the result and consequence of God's work. But if they are the result and consequence, it seems fair to conclude that these works aren't the basis but the evidence and proof of new life; they testify to the Spirit's presence in one's life.

Another text that accords with the theme pursued here is Ephesians 2:8–10: "For by grace you have been saved through faith. And this is not your own doing; it is the gift of God, not a result of works, so that no one may boast. For we are his workmanship, created in Christ Jesus for good works, which God prepared beforehand, that we should walk in them." Here we see the theme that has occupied us in this book. Salvation can't be gained by works—all human boasting in what we have achieved or done is excluded. And yet we are "created . . . for good works." Three features of good works should be noted here. First, the term "workmanship" (*poiēma)* refers to "the works of divine creation" (e.g., Rom. 1:20; Testament of Job 49:2–3).[7] The works are the product of God's work, of his creative power. Second, this is reaffirmed in the words "created in Christ Jesus," demonstrating that the works believers do flow from the new creation that has dawned in Jesus Christ. Third, these works are planned in advance by God, representing what he has ordained, arranged, and prepared for those who belong to him.

When we actually read what Paul says about good works, we see that he is remarkably similar to James! Good works are necessary for justification, but they aren't the basis of justification since God is infinitely holy and all people fall short of his glory. Still, good works provide evidence that one has received

7. Walter Bauer, *A Greek-English Lexicon of the New Testament and Other Early Christian Literature,* rev. and ed. Frederick William Gingrich, 3rd ed. (Chicago: University of Chicago Press, 2000), s.v. "ποίημα."

the grace of God, that the Spirit is working in one's life. Our good works are accepted in Christ, as Calvin remarks,

> Therefore, as we ourselves, when we have been engrafted into Christ, are righteous in God's sight because our iniquities are covered by Christ's sinlessness, so our works are righteous and are thus regarded because whatever fault is otherwise in them is buried in Christ's purity, and is not charged to our account. . . . By faith alone not only we ourselves but our works as well are justified.[8]

Conclusion

In this chapter we have conducted a brief foray into the realm of systematic theology, giving attention to what Paul says about justification as it relates to the whole of Scripture and other doctrines. We saw that union with Christ is the overarching category in Paul's soteriology, so that justification fits within the orbit of participation in Christ. Justification is also correlated with many other salvific realities in Paul such as redemption, reconciliation, adoption, sanctification, and others. A striking convergence exists among all these different ways of describing God's work in Christ.

In every instance, the grace of God is featured so that salvation is clearly of the Lord. There is no suggestion that human works or achievement accomplish salvation. Instead, all the metaphors impress on us the miraculous and powerful work of the Lord in rescuing sinners from destruction and eternal misery. In this sense, justification is parallel with other soteric realities. This raises the question whether justification stands out in a particular way—if it is distinct from other soteriological benefits, and here we saw that justification explains with

8. Calvin, *Institutes*, 3:17:10 (1:813). Graham Cole suggested this citation from Calvin to me.

particular clarity that a right relationship with God doesn't depend on works but is received by faith. The contrast between works and faith is featured in justification in a way that is only paralleled by what Paul says about salvation. Furthermore, the Pauline teaching on justification explains the basis of a person being counted as righteous in God's sight, as Paul explains in a number of texts that Christ's death on the cross satisfied the wrath of God. In the cross God's righteousness is both saving and judging so that we see in the cross the holiness and love of God. Paul's teaching of justification helps us understand the cross with particular clarity.

We also considered the role of good works in justification, asking whether Paul and James stand apart in this matter. The picture painted in Paul might surprise many when it is unveiled. Paul, like James, also stresses that good works are necessary for final justification, for receiving life eternal. Indeed, the number of texts where Paul emphasizes the importance of good works, even Romans, 1–2 Corinthians, and Galatians, far exceeds what we might expect from many typical or popular treatments of Paul. Good works are indeed necessary, yet they are not a necessary *basis* but the necessary *consequence* of new life in Christ. Good works are the result of the powerful and transforming work of the Holy Spirit, the manifestation of the new creation that has dawned in Jesus Christ as the one who has triumphed over death. Thus, good works in Paul, as in James, function as the evidence and proof that one has new life in Christ. They can't be the basis since God demands perfection and believers still struggle with sin. Thus, the good works reveal the new orientation of the heart, but their imperfection is a token of the now and not yet character of salvation.

Epilogue

A Final Word

In this book I have defended the classic Reformed view that justification is by faith alone, that justification is forensic, that sinners are declared to be in the right on the basis of the penal substitutionary death of Christ, that the righteousness of Christ is imputed to us, and that works are a necessary evidence of justification. We have seen from the Old Testament, the teaching of Jesus, the epistles of Paul, and the rest of the New Testament that vindication, acquittal, and forgiveness are a gift of God. Salvation—including justification—is of the Lord!

What difference does the truth articulated and defended in this book make? Is it merely an academic jousting match between Protestants and Roman Catholics? Certainly not! The issue is how we can stand righteous before a holy God, and thus the matter is of the greatest importance since it has to do with our eternal salvation. I suspect that all who believe in the triune God would agree that understanding the truth about our relationship with him isn't trivial but speaks to one of the most important questions of life: how can I have peace with God?

The case I have made is that we enjoy peace with God through faith in Jesus Christ so that our righteousness before God is not based on what we do. When we come to know this truth, we are filled with assurance and comfort since justification is fundamentally God's work and not ours. We don't rest in ourselves and what we have done but in God's promise that those who rely on Christ crucified and risen stand in the right before him. When the devil comes and frightens us with our sins and failings, or when we tremble in fear as we think of the evil that we have perpetrated, we look to Christ and lean upon him for our righteousness. We can say to the devil and to our own conscience, you are absolutely right. I deserve to be condemned, for I am a sinner in thought, in word, and in deed. But there is no condemnation since I am united to Christ by faith (Rom. 8:1). No one can condemn me on the last day since God is the one who justifies me (Rom. 8:33). Yes, Jesus died and was raised on my behalf; he sits at the Father's right hand and intercedes for me based on his atoning sacrifice (Rom. 8:34). Thus, I find my assurance not in myself, not in my feelings, not in my performance, not even finally in my faith, but in Christ himself, my Savior and my God.

Justification by faith alone makes a difference because it gives us assurance, frees us from fear, and awakens praise in our hearts. Graham Cole, one of the editors of this volume, responded to me by writing, "Without justification by faith, salvation effectively becomes probation, and assurance disappears." When we realize that we have been rescued from death and destruction by one who loves us, when we contemplate what we deserved and see the love and kindness that freed us from a terrible fate, then we are thankful. We are filled with unspeakable and glorious joy, and we give thanks and praise to our great God—the Father, the Son, and the Spirit. In the economy of salvation, the Father planned our salvation, the Son came and won our salvation, and the Spirit applies this great work of salvation to our hearts.

Some people complain that justification is legal and cold and impersonal, but perhaps they have never experienced what it is like to have a judge say "not guilty" when prison and certain death loom before them. Perhaps they haven't sensed the trembling fear that exists when we stand before the Holy One of Israel, knowing that we are guilty. What relief, what joy, what exultation, and what glad and holy fear come when we hear the absolving verdict! And we tremble all the more when we realize that we don't deserve to be acquitted, and that we, though unworthy, have been the objects of God's great love. Nothing is hidden from him about us—our worst thoughts, our cruelest words, our most despicable actions—and yet he loves us and has pronounced the verdict that sends our souls soaring: justified!

Further Reading

Barrett, Matthew, ed. *The Doctrine on Which the Church Stands or Falls: Justification in Biblical, Theological, Historical, and Pastoral Perspective*. Wheaton, IL: Crossway, 2019. A valuable resource on the doctrine of justification.

Beilby, James K., and Paul Rhodes Eddy, eds. *Justification: Five Views*. Downers Grove, IL: IVP Academic, 2011. A helpful survey of various views of justification.

Bird, Michael F. *The Saving Righteousness of God: Studies on Paul, Justification, and the New Perspective*. Eugene, OR: Wipf and Stock, 2009. Bird represents a mediating view between the new perspective and more traditional understandings of justification.

Horton, Michael. *Justification*. 2 vols. Grand Rapids, MI: Zondervan Academic, 2018. An outstanding work on the doctrine of justification. Volume 1 surveys the historical teaching, and in volume 2 Horton works out his own biblical and theological understanding.

Piper, John. *The Future of Justification: A Response to N. T. Wright*. Wheaton, IL: Crossway, 2017. The title tells all as Piper responds to Wright's understanding of justification.

Schreiner, Thomas R. *Faith Alone: The Doctrine of Justification. What the Reformers Taught . . . and Why It Still Matters*. Grand Rapids, MI: Zondervan Academic, 2015. What can I say? It is a favorite in our family.

Seifrid, Mark A. *Christ, Our Righteousness: Paul's Theology of Justification*. NSBT 9. Downers Grove, IL: IVP Academic, 2000. A vigorous defense of the notion that our righteousness is in Christ crucified and risen.

Vickers, Brian. *Justification by Grace through Faith: Finding Freedom from Legalism, Lawlessness, Pride, and Despair*. Phillipsburg, NJ: P&R, 2013. An excellent theological and pastoral resource.

Westerholm, Stephen. *Justification Reconsidered: Rethinking a Pauline Theme*. Grand Rapids, MI: Eerdmans, 2013. A masterful analysis of recent proposals on justification.

Wright, N. T. *Justification: God's Plan and Paul's Vision*. Downers Grove, IL: IVP Academic, 2016. A fine introduction to Wright's distinctive understanding of justification.

General Index

Scripture and Ancient Sources Index